You Are The Temple

A 21st century apostle

    looks at the church

        through Ephesians

By John Krhin

Copyright © 2010 by John Krhin

You Are The Temple
A 21st century apostle looks at the church through Ephesians
by John Krhin

Printed in the United States of America

ISBN 9781612155005

All rights reserved solely by the author. The author guarantees all contents are original and do not infringe upon the legal rights of any other person or work. No part of this book may be reproduced in any form without the permission of the author. The views expressed in this book are not necessarily those of the publisher.

Unless otherwise indicated, Bible quotations are taken from The New King James Version. Copyright © 1982 by Thomas Nelson, Inc. Used by permission.

All illustrations have been taken from "free clipart" websites with ownership unidentified.

www.xulonpress.com

Contents

Acknowledgments vii

Preface ix

Introduction xxxv

Chapter 1   The Foundation 39

Chapter 2   Doctrine 45

"Heavenly places and Beyond"

Chapter 3   Your Position in Christ 54

Chapter 4   Grace and the Church 70

Chapter 5   Walking in Your Calling 74

Chapter 6   Government is Divine 78

Chapter 7   Death and Humility, part I 97

Chapter 8   Starving Our Apostles and Prophets 101

Chapter 9   Death and Humility, part II 107

Chapter 10	Consider Your calling	117
Chapter 11	Circumventing the Call of God	126
Chapter 12	The Mini-Church Movement	131
Chapter 13	What Does a Christian Look Like?	138
Chapter 14	Marriage is Where it's At	145
Chapter 15	We are in a War	161
Chapter 16	Postscript, a final look at the Ephesian church	182
Endnotes		189

Acknowledgments

I dedicate this book to my wife Julie for her continued faithfulness and encouragement while answering the call of God to the ministry. She has lived what I am trying to convey.

I would also like to thank Marlene Horn for her grammatical assistance and editing skills.

To all my brothers and sisters who have willingly followed the Holy Spirit's leading as we endeavor to walk in New Testament patterns, thank you.

Of course, I give all praise to "Jesus Christ the same yesterday, and today, and forever". Hebrews 13:8 Because He is the "faithful and true witness", we can confidently follow him as He builds His church.

Preface

Yes, I'm an apostle. In many circles, "them's fightin words." Another immediate response is, "Sorry, there were only twelve of those." Some actually think, "What kind of an ego trip is he on." Using the "A" word conjures up many other responses that will be addressed as I develop this topic. Hopefully your interest is captured just enough to make you continue reading.

Shortly after God called me into the ministry (the mid 1970's) a startling reality became apparent to me. The church was languishing...yes, the church that I was baptized into through the new birth.

Raised in Roman Catholicism, my wife and I were encouraged by our bishop (believe it or not!) in 1974 to leave parish life and join a church that would support our newfound faith...a church that believed in the authority of scripture. And so we joined the local Assembly of God. We immediately flourished in this new garden, but then reality moved in. We began to see that born-again, Spirit-filled Christians could be meaner and more messed up than people we knew in our Catholic life. Division, fruitless living and non-Biblical patterns were present in our new community of faith. In fact, I eventually would learn that this was the transdenominational norm. This was no brilliant observation on my part, but rather common knowledge, particularly among frustrated leaders in ministry. Stories such as the pastor who nightly drove to town's edge to witness the passing of a locomotive typified this frustration. Experiencing something he didn't have to push brought great exhilaration.

Working towards ordination involved finishing bible school, practical internship, staff ministry, and then leading a church plant. Ultimately I adopted the ministry philosophy derived from Ephesians 4:11-16. I now understood that I was to equip the saints for the work of the ministry, even though most of them preferred that I do the ministry and leave them alone. More often than I care to admit, I contributed to the problem.

When I first sat down to write this book over 25 years ago, I thought that I had many of the answers. And perhaps I had some. At various junctures I have believed that someone else, more qualified, should be doing this. But since then, while gaining confidence in Christ's calling upon my life as an apostle, I have come to believe that Jesus has it all under control. I have grown to love the church that Christ is yet building. And, I have committed my life to serve Him in this process. As He has called me to labor with Him, I am continually amazed by His love for the church.

Understanding and appreciating apostolic grace will greatly enhance your interaction with this writing because it is given primarily from that perspective. I arrived at a place in my life where I have come to grips with the apostolic stigma. This involves both the internal insecurities connected with answering the apostolic call and the external pressures, especially from the church, which resists the fact of this gift of grace in our day just as it has in every generation of church history. I am encouraged in this process by "...considering the Apostle and High Priest of our confession, Christ Jesus" (Hebrews 3:1), and by pondering the testimony of the apostle Paul in 1 Corinthians 15:9-10.

For I am the least of the apostles, who am not worthy to be called an apostle, because I persecuted the church of God. But by the grace of God I am what I am, and His grace toward me was not in vain; but I labored more abundantly than they all, yet not I, but the grace of God *which was* with me.

Only Jesus establishes the ministry gifts in the church (Ephesians 4:11). "And He Himself gave some *to be* apostles, some prophets, some evangelists, and some pastors and teachers". To Him we must all give an account.

"For *the kingdom of heaven is* like a man traveling to a far country, *who* called his own servants and delivered his goods to them. And to one he gave five talents, to another two, and to another one, to each according to his own ability; and immediately

he went on a journey. Then he who had received the five talents went and traded with them, and made another five talents. And likewise he who *had received* two gained two more also. But he who had received one went and dug in the ground, and hid his lord's money. After a long time the lord of those servants came and settled accounts with them.

"So he who had received five talents came and brought five other talents, saying, 'Lord, you delivered to me five talents; look, I have gained five more talents besides them.' His lord said to him, 'Well *done,* good and faithful servant; you were faithful over a few things, I will make you ruler over many things. Enter into the joy of your lord.' He also who had received two talents came and said, 'Lord, you delivered to me two talents; look, I have gained two more talents besides them.' His lord said to him, 'Well *done,* good and faithful servant; you have been faithful over a few things, I will make you ruler over many things. Enter into the joy of your lord.'

"Then he who had received the one talent came and said, 'Lord, I knew you to be a hard man, reaping where you have not sown, and gathering where you have not scattered seed. And I was afraid, and went and hid your talent in the ground. Look, *there* you have *what is* yours.'

"But his lord answered and said to him, 'You wicked and lazy servant, you knew that I reap where I have not sown, and gather where I have not scattered seed. So you ought to have deposited my money with the bankers, and at my coming I would have received back my own with interest. So take the talent from him, and give *it* to him who has ten talents. 'For to everyone who has, more will be given, and he will have abundance; but from him who does not have, even what he has will be taken away. And cast the unprofitable servant into the outer darkness. There will be weeping and gnashing of teeth." Matthew 25:14-30

"For we must all appear before the judgment seat of Christ, that each one may receive the things *done* in the body, according to what he has done, whether good or bad." 2 Corinthians 5:10

As Paul considered his stewardship, the stigmata that he testified of in Galatians 6:17 were a direct expression of his fellowship with Christ's sufferings (Philippians 3:7-14) and his call to be an apostle. The same stigma that accompanied Christ's call to apostleship is upon all those who allow His grace to labor through them. It may vary, but it is actually present with every gift of grace. Paul's encouragement to young Timothy explains this correlation of suffering with and for Christ in 2 Timothy 2:7-14.

"Consider what I say, and may the Lord give you understanding in all things.

Remember that Jesus Christ, of the seed of David, was raised from the dead according to my gospel, for which I suffer trouble as an evildoer, *even* to the point of chains; but the word of God is not chained. Therefore

I endure all things for the sake of the elect, that they also may obtain the salvation which is in Christ Jesus with eternal glory. *This is* a faithful saying: For if we died with *Him,*
We shall also live with *Him.* If we endure, We shall also reign with *Him.* If we deny *Him,* He also will deny us. If we are faithless, He remains faithful; He cannot deny Himself. Remind *them* of these things, charging *them* before the Lord not to strive about words to no profit, to the ruin of the hearers."

Just as Christ experienced suffering as the Apostle of our profession, all those who receive the gift of apostolic grace will experience a portion of that suffering. This on-going process is at the core of what I earlier referred to as "internal insecurities". Every one of us must work through this faith process.

For I say, through the grace given to me, to everyone who is among you, not to think *of himself* more highly than he ought to think, but to think soberly, as God has dealt to each one a measure of faith. For as we have many members in one body, but all the members do not have the same function, so we, *being* many, are one body in Christ, and individually members of one another. Having then gifts differing according to the grace that is given to us, *let us use them:* if prophecy, *let us prophesy* in proportion to our faith; or ministry, *let us use it* in *our* ministering; he who teaches, in teaching; he who exhorts, in exhortation; he who gives, with liberality; he who leads, with diligence; he who shows mercy, with cheerfulness. Romans 12:3-8

Peter concurs with Paul that humility and soberness must accompany our response to God's call.

"The elders who are among you I exhort, I who am a fellow elder and a witness of the sufferings of Christ, and also a partaker of the glory that will be revealed: Shepherd the flock of God which is among you, serving as overseers, not by compulsion but willingly, not for dishonest gain but eagerly; nor as being lords over those entrusted to you, but being examples to the flock; and when the Chief Shepherd appears, you will receive the crown of glory that does not fade away. Likewise you younger people, submit yourselves to *your* elders. Yes, all of *you* be submissive to one another, and be clothed with humility, for *"God resists the proud, But gives grace to the humble."* Therefore humble yourselves under the mighty hand of God, that He may exalt you in due time, casting all your care upon Him, for He cares for you.

Be sober, be vigilant; because your adversary the devil walks about like a roaring lion, seeking whom he may devour. Resist him, steadfast in the faith, knowing that the same sufferings are experienced by your brotherhood in the world. But may the God of all grace, who called us to His eternal glory by Christ Jesus, after you have suffered a while, perfect, establish, strengthen, and settle *you*. To Him *be*

the glory and the dominion forever and ever. Amen."
(1 Peter 5:1-14"

Satan himself plays on our insecurities. That is why we must "Resist him, steadfast in the faith". When Paul told king Agrippa that he **"...was not disobedient to the heavenly vision"** (Acts 26:19), he was testifying of his victory over all of his insecurities. Likewise, when he wrote to the Corinthians of Christ's words to him, "...My grace is sufficient for you, for My strength is made perfect in weakness." (2 Cor 12:9), he was testifying of his victory over pride.

Christ's call upon my life to be an apostle requires an on-going identification with His Apostleship, a willingness to be accountable to Him, and humble submission to His grace that works in me. If Paul saw himself as "the least of the apostles" (1 Cor 15:9), who by God's grace was able to answer that call, any others (including me) who receive the call of apostle must do the same.

Concerning my reference about the "external pressures" to the apostolic call, particularly from the church, I begin by offering my experience and observations. The church has consistently had difficulty embracing apostolic ministry both practically and structurally. Jesus was continually misunderstood by his disciples. Paul often found himself "defending" his apostolic ministry. The church either wants to exalt or defame its apostles. It seems there is no middle ground.

When Christ brought me to saving faith he called me out of the Catholic Church and into the Assemblies of God. As mentioned earlier, my new church environment was less than perfect. And so was my ability to "fit in", particularly as I answered the call to the ministry. I found that there was ample emphasis on pastoral and teaching ministry, limited attention to that of the evangelist, and virtually no mention of contemporary apostles and prophets...except in occasional demeaning or sarcastic references. This is peculiar, even alarming, considering that the church is built upon the foundation of the apostles and prophets (Ephesians 2:20).

Early on I wondered why I thought differently than many of my associates in ministry. Why did I struggle with the status quo? Why was I preoccupied with the urge to work with new groups of people and looking at fields beyond? Why was I prone to dogmatism? Why was I always calling others to consider ministry? Why was I frustrated with the lack of Holy Spirit power operating in our Pentecostal circles and in my own life? Why was I always examining church structure, longing for New Testament patterns? These were among a host of questions with which many of my peers didn't seem to struggle. In fact I at times found myself challenging what I perceived to be their lack of concern.

As time went by, connections with likeminded ministers began to develop. This led to team ministry and the concept of plurality of elders in our local church. Even though these changes began to take "the edge" off the struggle, our work had just begun. Interaction among the ministry gifts releases grace for the body to grow and in fact is a microcosm of what God intends for the entire church (Ephesians 4:16). Hence, I have endeavored to engage other ministers at every opportunity. The digression that follows is intended to explain: 1) why I continue to serve as an ordained minister of the gospel in the Assemblies of God, and 2) as an encouragement to fellow ministers in the A/G and other less-than-perfect fellowships.

The fact is: no denomination, fellowship, or individual has yet attained perfection. Because of this, the A/G (as other churches similarly do) prefaces its doctrinal positions within its Constitution with this statement.

> "The Bible is our all-sufficient rule for faith and practice. This Statement of Fundamental Truths is

intended simply as a basis of fellowship among us (i.e., that we all speak the same thing, 1 Corinthians 1:10; Acts 2:42). The phraseology employed in this statement is not inspired or contended for, but the truth set forth is held to be essential to a full-gospel ministry. No claim is made that it contains all biblical truth, only that it covers our need as to these fundamental doctrines."[i]

In the same Constitution, under Amendments, you will find this information.

"Amendments to the Constitution may be made at any regularly called session of the General Council provided that the proposed amendments have been submitted in writing at least 6 months in advance to the Executive Presbytery. Before the Executive Presbytery may submit proposed amendments for consideration by a session of the General Council, it shall provide written notice of the proposed amendments by regular mail to the office of each district superintendent and each district secretary, and by insertion in the Assemblies of God Ministers Letter or any successor publication sent periodically to ministers of The General Council of the Assemblies of God, not later than 60 days prior to said session. Amendments to the Constitution shall require a two-thirds vote of all members present and voting."[ii]

These statements illustrate that our doctrines affecting both faith and practice are subject to the Bible and that they can be addressed through due process. Though due process can be very cumbersome, the following texts indicate that this is both scriptural and reasonable.

"For who makes you differ *from another?* And what do you have that you did not receive? Now if you did indeed receive *it,* why do you boast as if you had not received *it?*" 1 Corinthians 4:7

"All Scripture *is* given by inspiration of God, and *is* profitable for doctrine, for reproof, for correction, for instruction in righteousness, that the man of God may be complete, thoroughly equipped for every good work." 2 Timothy 3:16

"...knowing this first, that no prophecy of Scripture is of any private interpretation, for prophecy never came by the will of man, but holy men of God spoke *as they were* moved by the Holy Spirit." 2 Peter 1:20-21

"And they continued steadfastly in the apostles' doctrine and fellowship...And certain *men* came down from Judea and taught the brethren, "Unless you are circumcised according to the custom of Moses, you cannot be saved." Therefore, when Paul and Barnabas had no small dissension and dispute with them, they determined that Paul and Barnabas and certain others of them should go up to Jerusalem, to the apostles and elders, about this question. So, being sent on their way by the church, they passed through Phoenicia and Samaria, describing the conversion of the Gentiles; and they caused great joy to all the brethren. And when they had come to Jerusalem, they were received by the church and the apostles and the elders; and they reported all things that God had done with them. But some of the sect of the Pharisees who believed rose up, saying, "It is necessary to circumcise them, and to command *them* to keep the law of Moses." Now the apostles and elders came together to consider this matter. And when there had been much dispute, Peter rose up *and* said to them: "Men *and* brethren, you know that a good while ago God chose among us, that by my mouth the Gentiles should hear the word of the gospel and believe. So God, who knows the heart, acknowledged them by giving them the Holy Spirit, just as *He did* to us, and made no distinction between us and them, purifying their hearts by faith. Now therefore, why do you test God by putting a yoke on the neck of the disciples which neither our fathers nor we were able to bear? But we believe that through the grace of the Lord Jesus Christ we shall be saved in the same manner as they." Then all the multitude kept silent and listened to Barnabas and Paul declaring how many miracles and wonders God had worked through them among the Gentiles. And after they had become silent, James answered, saying, "Men *and* brethren, listen to me: Simon has declared how God at the first visited the Gentiles to take out of them a people for His name. And with this the words of the prophets agree, just as it is written:

'After this I will return and will rebuild the tabernacle of David, which has fallen down; I will rebuild its ruins, And I will set it up; So that the rest of mankind may seek the LORD, Even all the Gentiles who are called by My name, Says the LORD who does all these things.' Known to God from eternity are all His works. Therefore I judge that we should not trouble those from among the Gentiles who are turning to God, but that we write to them to abstain from things polluted by idols, *from* sexual immorality, *from* things strangled, and *from* blood. For Moses has had throughout many generations those who preach him in every city, being read in the synagogues every Sabbath. Then it pleased the apostles and elders, with the whole church, to send chosen men of their own company to Antioch with Paul and Barnabas, *namely,* Judas who was also named Barsabas,

and Silas, leading men among the brethren. They wrote this, *letter* by them: 'The apostles, the elders, and the brethren, To the brethren who are of the Gentiles in Antioch, Syria, and Cilicia: Greetings. Since we have heard that some who went out from us have troubled you with words, unsettling your souls, saying, "*You must* be circumcised and keep the law"—to whom we gave no *such* commandment—it seemed good to us, being assembled with one accord, to send chosen men to you with our beloved Barnabas and Paul, men who have risked their lives for the name of our Lord Jesus Christ. We have therefore sent Judas and Silas, who will also report the same things by word of mouth. For it seemed good to the Holy Spirit, and to us, to lay upon you no greater burden than these necessary things: that you abstain from things offered to idols, from blood, from things strangled, and from sexual immorality. If you keep yourselves from these, you will do well. Farewell.'

So when they were sent off, they came to Antioch; and when they had gathered the multitude together, they delivered the letter. When they had read it, they rejoiced over its encouragement. Now Judas and Silas, themselves being prophets also, exhorted and strengthened the brethren with many words. And after they had stayed *there* for a time, they were sent back with greetings from the brethren to the apostles. However, it seemed good to Silas to remain there. Paul and Barnabas also remained in Antioch, teaching and preaching the word of the Lord, with many others also.

Then after some days Paul said to Barnabas, "Let us now go back and visit our brethren in every city where we have preached the word of the Lord, *and see* how they are doing." Now Barnabas was determined to take with them John called Mark. But

Paul insisted that they should not take with them the one who had departed from them in Pamphylia, and had not gone with them to the work. Then the contention became so sharp that they parted from one another. And so Barnabas took Mark and sailed to Cyprus; but Paul chose Silas and departed, being commended by the brethren to the grace of God. And he went through Syria and Cilicia, strengthening the churches." Acts 2:42; 15:1-41

"Now I plead with you, brethren, by the name of our Lord Jesus Christ, that you all speak the same thing, and *that* there be no divisions among you, but *that* you be perfectly joined together in the same mind and in the same judgment." 1 Corinthians 1:10

When I say that practically and structurally the church does not know how to embrace apostolic ministry, I see it as a problem rooted in church government, dogma, and tradition. We have created systems that have a hard time responding to change. Nonetheless, we must embrace change as the new wine skins Jesus suggested us to be. Or we will lose both the wine and the wine skins.

Within the Assemblies of God, apostolic ministry is understood from a variety of perspectives. To begin with, our doctrinal statement references "The Ministry" as such:

> "A divinely called and scripturally ordained ministry has been provided by our Lord for the threefold purpose of leading the Church in: (1) evangelization of the world (Mark 16:15-20), (2) worship of God (John 4:23,24), and (3) building a Body of saints being perfected in the image of His Son (Ephesians 4:11,16)."

Inherent in this description of "The Ministry" is the last reference to Ephesians 4:11,16. Verse 11 is a list of the ministry gifts commonly referred to as the five-fold ministry, "And He Himself gave some *to be* apostles, some prophets, some evangelists, and some pastors and teachers." Verse 16 describes the resulting process when these ministry gifts interact with all other members of the church.

"From whom the whole body, joined and knit together by what every joint supplies, according to the effective working by which every part does its share, causes growth of the body for the edifying of itself in love."

Context (verses 7-15) indicates that the ministry gifts of verse 11 are to equip or prepare the saints for the work of the ministry.

"But to each one of us grace was given according to the measure of Christ's gift. Therefore He says:
'When He ascended on high, He led captivity captive, And gave gifts to men.'
(Now this, *"He ascended"*—what does it mean but that He also first descended into the lower parts of the earth? [10] He who descended is also the One who ascended far above all the heavens, that He might fill all things.) And He Himself gave some *to be* apostles, some prophets, some evangelists, and some pastors and teachers, for the equipping of the saints for the work of ministry, for the edifying of the body of Christ, till we all come to the unity of the faith and of the knowledge of the Son of God, to a perfect man, to the measure of the stature of the fullness of Christ; that we should no longer be children, tossed to and fro and carried about with every wind of doctrine, by the trickery of men, in the cunning

craftiness of deceitful plotting, but, speaking the truth in love, may grow up in all things into Him who is the head—Christ—

The A/G Bylaws also include by name the Ephesian 4:11 ministry gifts under the section "Ministry Described", followed by the statement, "We understand God's call to these ministry gifts is totally within His sovereign discretion without regard to gender, race, disability, or national origin".

Specifically, and as recently as 2003, the following "Operational Definition" concerning "Apostolic Ministry and the U.S. Assemblies of God" appeared in the Minutes of the 50th Session of The General Council of the Assemblies of God.

"The general superintendent presented a statement adopted by the Executive Presbytery regarding the subject of Apostolic Ministry and the U.S. Assemblies of God. He stated that it is the desire of the Executive Presbytery that this statement be in the hands of every Assemblies of God minister." The statement as presented follows:

"The Executive Presbytery adopted the following as an operational definition in regard to Apostolic Ministry and the U.S. Assemblies of God.

'Biblical apostolic ministry is marked by God-sent, church-recognized leaders whose ministry, through the anointed proclamation of the gospel, with accompanying signs and wonders, results in the expansion of the kingdom of God.'

Biblical Apostolic leadership as demonstrated by the Early Church...

- Depends totally on the enduement of the Holy Spirit's power for the release of His supernatural gifts.
- Extends the borders of the kingdom of God through penetrating and impacting unevangelized and unreached people groups with the gospel.
- Develops enduring relationships through mentoring.
- Enlists, equips, empowers, and releases new generations of leaders.
- Plants and develops healthy local self-supporting and reproducing New Testament congregations.
- Produces lasting fruitfulness through the continuous multiplication of New Testament congregations.
- Models spiritual responsibility, accountability, and humility, aspiring to neither title nor office.
- A suggestion was made that when this statement is issued that it include also the phrase, 'depends totally on the Word of God.'[iii]

However, because the Assemblies of God and other denominations/fellowships that consider these issues are operating from a governmental and doctrinal framework that is still not wholly biblical...apostles, prophets, and even evangelists have difficulty fitting into that framework.

Fortunately the final verdict has not yet been decided. Change is still occurring even though it is at times agonizingly slow. We do not have to go the route of denominational history that is replete with examples of wine skins that have burst. Our fellowship can still be among the front-runners of Pentecostal church life, both practically and structurally. The "apostolic revolution" occurring with the Assemblies of God in Australia is a case in point. They have begun a process that is radically addressing this and related issues.

I have not kept current with its development, but I believe they have taken steps that other segments of our movement have neglected to address. Other fellowships/denominations throughout the world are experiencing dynamic results by embracing apostles and prophets. I urge the Assemblies of God in the USA to do so as well. We are behind the curve on this one. It is time for a proliferation of local, regional, and even national dialogues addressing this topic.

Today, scaffolding can be seen which supports frantic crews using humanistic methods and materials in futile attempts to refurbish decaying denominational structures or to create new ones in an attempt to house the church of the living God. At first glance the project appears to be progressing successfully. Strong new arches and beautiful lines accent the building. Huge amounts of money and man-hours are producing results that outwardly shine and draw attention. But I dare say that much of this effort could be compared to the picture of hypocrisy that Jesus spoke of in Matthew 23:27, "...For you are like whitewashed tombs which indeed appear beautiful outwardly, but inside are full of dead *men's* bones and all uncleanness."

On the other hand, Jesus is indeed building His church, the True Church, a structure that will last forever. He is vitally concerned with the condition of our building process, not just the outward appearance. According to Ephesians 5:27, He will one day, "**...present her to Himself a glorious church, not having spot or wrinkle or any such thing, but that she should be holy and without blemish.**"

In the early 1980's David Wilkerson indicated that the great missionary thrust of the future would be spearheaded by Third World ministers who would go to the field at a fraction of the expense required by the western church. This is happening because they have not yet been over-structured and steeped in tradition, though the signs are there. In 2005 I had the glorious experience of accompanying one of our evangelists to India. We had the privilege of seeing over 5,000 commitments to Christ over a ten-day period. Healings were abundant. However the greatest impact on me was meeting two Indian "pastors". My perception was that they are actually apostles. One of them served as the crusade director for the evangelist. He performed that role admirably. But together with a team of evangelists, other pastors, and student ministers, he is spearheading an effort to plant a church in every village of their province. The other man, who is not affiliated with the Assemblies of God, pastors a church of over 2,000 members. But more significantly he leads an effort that has planted over 200 churches in the last 25 years.

Most readers of this book will probably agree that God uses Spirit-anointed people to build his church and reach the world with the gospel of Jesus Christ. Are we willing to adjust our structure in an on-going way that will accommodate the fullness of God's gifted ministers?

"Therefore He says:
   "When He ascended on high,
   He led captivity captive,
   And gave gifts to men."
And He Himself gave some *to be* **apostles, some prophets, some evangelists, and some pastors and teachers,** [12] **for the equipping of the saints for the work of ministry, for the edifying of the body of Christ."**
(Ephesians 4:8,11-12).

I humbly pray that this writing will reflect the work of Jesus rather than a criticism of men's means and methods. If I had completed the composition at an earlier date, I am afraid that it would have concentrated on the latter rather than the former. Perhaps you are familiar with the process of training money handlers to recognize the counterfeit. I am told that concentrating on the authentic is what best helps one to spot the false. I have endeavored to edit my work to reflect this methodology. Even though reference must be made to what is false and to men's failures, please accept this effort as an attempt to identify the true work of Jesus in the world today. Hopefully all who read this can use it as a helpful tool in understanding Christ's Church…that mystery revealed in the New Testament. To all who are a part, God says…You Are The Temple.

Introduction

When I first returned to Duluth, MN in 1980 to serve as the founding pastor of what has eventually become Living Stones Fellowship "House of Refuge" (Duluth) and "House of Praise" (Side Lake), I was not prepared for the revelations that would begin to unfold. Like most other young, zealous "church planters", I was encouraged by the opportunity. After all, I would be starting with a core group of Christians; seed money was available, we were able to acquire a church building; and the pastor who led me to Christ was serving the church that was mothering us.

At this point let me be careful to state that the following revelations are in no way intended to place blame on any individual or view. They are only my observations intended to set a framework with which some later suggestions might be compared.

What were some of these revelations? First, there were several different views within our core group about why and how we should proceed. Some of the people were not content (at times openly critical) concerning the direction that our mother church was taking. Now, mind you, these were not in agreement. One party believed we should return to a more traditional Assemblies of God approach to church life. Another party was convinced that a contemporary, even progressive path was the way to go. Interestingly, both expressed the desire to remain as a smaller, relationally orientated church. Secondly, there were very strong convictions about marriage and divorce, church government, worship, small group ministry…to name a few subjects. Thirdly, but not last, it would be revealed toward the end of our first year that some of the core group would be returning to our mother church after that period of time. Other, not necessarily less significant revelations, came to light on an on-going basis. But suffice it to say that potential pandemonium was in the air.

We were part of the greater church planting/church growth movement that was catching on throughout our nation and which had been "reaping" a harvest in the wake of the charismatic renewal. In the first several years of our church plant, over one thousand visitors (many who were leaving other churches in pursuit of their ideal) passed through our doors. In fact, during the first five years of our efforts, I know of at least between ten and fifteen other church plants that were attempted in our community of about 100,000 people. So ours was not an isolated story. It was being replicated in many communities throughout the land. Perhaps you were in one of them! I am sure you could tell me a few stories of your own.

Before this church plant I had the opportunity to serve under four different pastors who had accumulated well over 100 years of pastoral experience. In addition, my years at North Central Bible College witnessed a changing of the guard. It was a blessing to be exposed to such a rich diversity of experience and ministry styles. Some of the staff shared experiences from before World War II as first generation Pentecostal descendents of Azusa Street, Topeka, and other similar visitations. Others were fresh out of seminaries, loaded with the latest insights and methods. All were men and women of God, devoted to the scriptures, and advocates of New Testament Pentecostal ministry. Even though none of them talked practically about apostles and prophets, there was an emphasis from some on equipping the saints.

But now I was on my own. Welcome to the ministry! Pastoral theology had only slightly prepared me for pastor/board dynamics. I clung to one of my professor's remarks. "Any church problem may find a solution through a timely death, resignation, or departure". But these things did not come fast enough. And the congregation was stuck with me!

What were other ministers doing? Sharing experiences with them helped some, as did occasional seminars and retreats. But, more often than not, these gatherings caused many to return home filled with ideas and practices that seemingly were bringing results elsewhere. After a while, when the same results were not achieved in their situation, there would be a return to the status quo until the next new trend was popularized.

Again and again I came back to the same answer: we must experience more of the elements of primitive New Testament church life. Of course I was far from the first young idealistic minister to form such a conclusion. And to some degree any sincere Christian will long for experiences read about in the New Testament.

Acts 2:40-47 contains prime examples of what the church should include: power evangelism, fellowship, discipleship, doctrine, worship, and prayer. Though most would agree that these are among the vital aspects towards which we should aspire, application of them includes great variety and potential for disagreement. Paul's letter to the Ephesians provides important insights upon which New Testament church life can be built. These will be presented at length in later chapters. Before this, and if you have identified with the brief history that I have shared with you, please keep reading. It may revolutionize your life and ministry.

Chapter 1

The Foundation

A sure foundation makes for a secure beginning, a steady building process, and an established end result. After being involved with several home remodeling and building projects, I can verify that success requires a sure foundation. If it is not done at the onset, or if the foundation deteriorates, the superstructure will be greatly compromised.

Today, the church's foundation continually needs to be laid, repaired, and in some instances rebuilt. This alone justifies the need for a modern understanding of apostolic and prophetic ministry, according to Ephesians 2:19-22, which describes the church building process.

> Now, therefore, you are no longer strangers and foreigners, but fellow citizens with the saints and members of the household of God, having been built

on the foundation of the apostles and prophets, Jesus Christ Himself being the chief corner*stone, in whom the whole building, being fitted together, grows into a holy temple in the Lord, in whom you also are being built together for a dwelling place of God in the Spirit.*

God is a builder. We are the building. Is a foundation needed any less today than when the church began? When Abraham "looked for a city which hath foundations" (Hebrews 11:10), he prophetically hungered for what we now are experiencing as stated in Ephesians 2:19-22. In fact, the worldwide resurgence of apostolic and prophetic ministers bears witness to the fact that Jesus is sticking to His building plan. With this comes a process of self-examination as well.

"For the time *has come* for judgment to begin at the house of God..." (1 Peter 4:17a). "*...Yet once more I shake not only the earth, but also heaven.*" Now this, *"Yet once more,"* indicates the removal of those things that are being shaken, as of things that are made, that the things which cannot be shaken may remain. (Hebrews 12:26(b)-27).

We should be greatly encouraged to know that Jesus said, "...I will build My church, and the gates of

Hades shall not prevail against it." (Matthew 16:18b). However, the apostle Paul told Timothy that, "... in a great house there are not only vessels of gold and silver, but also of wood and clay, some for honor and some for dishonor." (1 Timothy 2:20).

I have observed that we have a tremendous capacity to build apart from God. At Babel they said, "Come, let us build ourselves a city, and a tower whose top *is* in the heavens; let us make a name for ourselves, lest we be scattered abroad over the face of the whole earth." (Genesis 11:4). Much of what is built upon this earth, physically and organizationally has nothing at all to do with God's inspiration. Our renowned architectural, political, and economic giants are testimonies of human ingenuity. This carries over into the church as well. We are prone to build with much ingenuity under a religious guise. In fact, the ultimate religious effort will be a self-perpetuating heap of false building. "For the time will come when they will not endure sound doctrine, but according to their own desires, *because* they have itching ears, they will heap up for themselves teachers." (II Timothy 4:3).

When explaining the building process, Paul stated that "each one's work will become clear..." (I Corinthians 3:13). He also exhorted that " As you therefore have received Christ Jesus the Lord, so walk in Him, rooted and built up in Him... Let no one cheat you of your reward... and not holding fast to the Head, from whom all the body... grows with the increase *that is* from God." (Colossians 2:6-7,18-19 excerpts).

We (the church) are not only now a building under construction, inhabited by God through the Spirit. We shall be the bride, the Lamb's wife, that holy city in which the Lord God Almighty and the Lamb are the temple. Amazingly though, much (most?) of the church today is not practically conscious of the fact that we are "under construction" upon the foundation of Jesus Christ. Why? It is because so many lives are built around Christ, not on Christ.

This book will show that the church is a people who comprise the ultimate dwelling place of God. We need the same spirit of revelation that New Testament writers were given. Then we will be better equipped to look on the inward rather than the outward. We will be more clearly able to see why God selected David or the apostles. God looked upon David's heart, not his stature. We in turn need to look on the inward as well.

The first apostles were uneducated. They were not from among the religious hierarchy. However, we too often ordain ministers based on intellectual qualifications, organizational skills, communicative abilities, etc. Even physical visage and deportment come into play. This carries into everyday church life as well. It is the businessman, professional, or skilled worker who is nominated to serve as a deacon or trustee. Other positions and plans are filled or pursued via humanistic reasoning and worldly models. Success is too often equated with size and numbers.

So, of what should the church's foundation be comprised? **"For no other foundation can anyone lay than that which is laid, which is Jesus Christ."** (1 Corinthia_ns 3:11). Jesus, the Christ, is the foundation. And He is also the builder (it will be explained later how the designation of Jesus as the Christ will greatly affect the building process). **"Unless the LORD builds the house, They labor in vain who build it..."** (Psalm 127:1). Paul summarized this building process by calling himself a wise master builder (also one who planted)...Apollos was referred to as one who watered...all of us as laborers together with God.

Not only is the foundation of Christ essential, but the process itself is foundational. Paul was given grace to lay foundations. He was doing what the apostles and prophets were "graced" to do as quoted earlier in Ephesians 2:19-22.

Apostles and prophets are foundational ministries, gifted to build foundations, gifted to perfect the saints at every phase of the building process. This is their role in the Ephesians 4:7-16 description of the church's development.

From this understanding of foundations (Christ the chief cornerstone and the apostles and prophets as foundational ministries) a natural extrapolation can be made. Foundations must be laid under all segments of life and structure in the church, beginning with the personal faith and walk of the believer, then encompassing church government, family, stewardship, spiritual gifts and ministries, doctrine, relationships, spiritual warfare, prayer, evangelism...ad infinitum. Every conceivable area of life and structure within the building process of the church requires foundations. Thank God that an ever increasing portion of the body of Christ is recognizing this need and is responding to apostolic and prophetic ministries which are building foundations upon Christ. Our generation is witnessing both the laying of new foundations through a proliferation of church planting and a renovation of previously existing church structures that are willing to respond.

Out of all the possible areas that require foundations several will be discussed in the following chapters in order to illustrate our need to address this topic today. The foundations in these areas are neglected, corrupted or destroyed throughout the church. And all of them certainly fall within the category addressed by Psalms 11:3 and 82:5 "If the foundations are destroyed, what can the righteous do? They do not know, nor do they understand; They walk about in darkness; All the foundations of the earth are unstable."

As these verses are found in contexts discussing righteousness, wickedness and God's judgment, the subjects discussed below must also be examined in such contexts for they are under the judgment of God. "For the time *has come* for judgment to begin at the house of God; and if *it begins* with us first, what will *be* the end of those who do not obey the gospel of God?" (1 Peter 4:17)? Let us look first at the foundation of doctrine.

Chapter 2

Doctrine

"Beloved, while I was very diligent to write to you concerning our common salvation, I found it necessary to write to you exhorting you to contend earnestly for the faith which was once for all delivered to the saints For certain men have crept in unnoticed, who long ago were marked out for this condemnation, ungodly men, who turn the grace of our God into lewdness and deny the only Lord God and our Lord Jesus Christ."
Jude 3,4

" Take heed to yourself and to the doctrine. Continue in them, for in doing this you will save both yourself and those who hear you." I Timothy 4:16

" And they continued steadfastly in the apostles' doctrine and fellowship, in the breaking of bread, and in prayers." Acts 2:42

Contrary to popular belief and preaching, there is a specific body of teaching that the New Testament refers to as the apostles' doctrine. This body of doctrine is absolutely essential to church order and life. Yet many voices incessantly downplay the importance of doctrine, relegating its discussion as potentially divisive, viewing dogma (formal proclamation of doctrine) as a Spirit-quenching evil. What a diabolical tragedy this is. New Testament doctrine, which is in measure is hard to be understood (II Peter 3:16), nevertheless is precise, knowable, and transferable (II Timothy 2:2). Why is it then that there is such resistance to so clear a message? Paul's words to the Ephesian elders say it well.

"For I have not shunned to declare unto you all the counsel of God... For I know this, that after my departure savage wolves will come in among you, not sparing the flock. Also from among yourselves men will rise up, speaking perverse things, to draw away the disciples after themselves." Acts 20:27, 29-30

Yes, we are often our worst enemies.

As stated earlier, man has a tremendous capacity to build apart from God. Paul taught Timothy, "As I urged you when I went into Macedonia—remain in Ephesus that you may charge some that they teach no other doctrine." I Timothy 1:3

So, what is sound doctrine? Hebrews 6:1-2 describes the foundations as "...repentance from dead works and of faith toward God, of the doctrine of baptisms, of laying on of hands, of resurrection of the dead, and of eternal judgment." These absolutes involve salvation, water baptism, the baptism in the Holy Spirit, Divine healing, dynamic faith, church ordinances, and eschatology. Yes, even eschatology should be precise and absolute. Today's varying postulations of how Christ is coming, when the dead are raised, and the manner of the millennium would have amazed the early apostles and prophets. Postulations are not foundations; sound doctrines are.

Salvation is by grace through faith, Ephesians 2:8. God does reward diligent faith, Hebrews 11:6. Believer's baptism by immersion is a proper command and mode, Mark 16:16; Acts 2:38,41. The baptism in the Holy Spirit was commanded by Jesus (Acts 1:4-5) and expected by the early church (Acts 8:14-17; 19:1-6). Divine healing and miracles were the norm (Acts 3:6-7; 4:30,33; 5:12,16; 6:8; 8:5-7). Laying on of hands was common (Mark 16:18; Acts 8:17; 19:6; James 5:14). The translation of the church, Jesus' personal return, and a literal millennial reign of Christ are a secure hope for the saints and an awesome warning to the unregenerate, Matthew 25:31-ff; Acts 1:11; I Corinthians 15:51-52; I Thessalonians 4:13-18; Titus 2:13-15; Revelation

20:4,11-15. Scripture then clearly indicates that godly, love-filled living with fruitful ministry are the goals of functional maturity, Ephesians 4:11-16; Hebrews 5:14.

Excesses, heresies, and vain imaginations continue to be prevalent and are exposed by the scriptures.

"If anyone teaches otherwise and does not consent to wholesome words, *even* the words of our Lord Jesus Christ, and to the doctrine which accords with godliness, he is proud, knowing nothing, but is obsessed with disputes and arguments over words, from which come envy, strife, reviling, evil suspicions, useless wranglings of men of corrupt minds and destitute of the truth, who suppose that godliness is a *means of gain*. From such withdraw yourself. Now godliness with contentment is great gain." I Timothy 6:3-6

"But there were also false prophets among the people, even as there will be false teachers among you, who will secretly bring in destructive heresies, even denying the Lord who bought them, *and* bring on themselves swift destruction. And many will follow their destructive ways, because of whom the way of truth will be blasphemed." II Peter 2:1-2

"Let no one cheat you of your reward, taking delight in *false* humility and worship of angels, intruding into those things which he has not seen, vainly puffed up by his fleshly mind, and not holding fast to the Head, from whom all the body, nourished and knit together by joints and ligaments, grows with the increase *that is* from God." Colossians 2:18-19

Because false teaching and practice occurred in the early church and continues today we must be prepared to establish and strengthen foundational doctrines.

The following expose illustrates how a harmful teaching affecting today's church can be corrected per the instructions of I Timothy 1:4-7; 4:1; 6:20 and II Timothy 2:1-26. Proper on-going presentation of good doctrine is the best prevention and cure for that which is error, I Timothy 1:3; 4:13,16 and II Timothy 2:1-2,15; 3:14-17; 4:2-3. The enemy of our souls would love to get us entangled with the latter at the expense of the former. Strong foundational doctrines will allow the church to be built according to the pattern and promise of Jesus.

It is well to remember that there is seldom any "new" error within the body of Christian teaching. A careful study of church history will show that the error discussed here has crept into the church before in one form or another. Also note that there are generally a few "key" errors from which many lesser ones spring forth. These indeed have a sound of truth because they use biblical phrases in their introduction and development.

The error to be addressed has often been referred to as "Manifested Sonship". It begins with the premise that revelation of knowledge is on-going. But an emphasis is made on "deeper" revelation "recently" made available to a select company of saints. This deeper revelation is a prominent characteristic of historic gnosticism which was addressed in the early church via John's gospel and epistles, Paul's letter to the Colossians, and Jude.

The error continues by teaching that Manifested Sons are coming forth today. These manifested sons will supposedly come into complete spiritual maturity before Jesus personally and literally returns to this earth. This "select company" will either establish The Millennium through their "sonship" and ruling as the body of Christ, or they will in effect bring the Kingdom of God to rule upon this earth through their influence. Jesus is then proposed to come. An extreme view is that this company's sonship is indeed the Second Coming of Christ. These approaches to eschatology are rehashed versions of amillennialism and postmillennialism. Connected as well with this error is the teaching that the five-fold ministry of Ephesians 4:11 are being restored during the end of the church age to perfect these manifest sons. Again, extremists have even demanded that this company "come out" or separate themselves in communities. This new order of the church is identified with the woman of Revelation 12. And the man child of that same chapter is a many-membered company identified as the manifested sons.

This particular false teaching was chosen for discussion because of its varied effect and influence upon the Pentecostal/Charismatic Movement of our day. Also, other valid topics discussed in this present writing have been maligned or shunned because of their supposed connection with this and other false teaching. This "throwing out the baby with the bath water" approach at times keeps the church from sincerely walking in truth. Similar trends can be seen in revivals where aberrant behavior and manifestations have caused God-intentioned effects of a revival to be dismissed. This is a reason that mainline churches initially rejected so much of the Modern Pentecostal Movement, and why in turn, many within the Modern Pentecostal Movement rejected so much of the Latter Rain and Charismatic Movements.

Now, as earlier outlined, teaching from some of the same texts cited in error can provide a source of strength for the church today. Let's begin with the term "manifested sons".

Romans 8:16-25 makes clear reference to them. But context declares that all true believers are sons of God. They shall become manifest or fully revealed when Jesus Christ personally returns for them at the resurrection and/or translation of the church (Romans 8:23-25; 1 Corinthians 15; 1 Thessalonians 4:13-18; 1 John 3:1-3; Revelation 20:1-6).

Jesus has given five major divisions of gifted men to equip his saints for ministry throughout the church age, Ephesians 4:11-16. Here "gave" is in the aorist tense, showing a completed action in the past tense. In other words, they are established ministries in the church. The ministry gifts of Ephesians 4:11 perfected the saints of the 1st Century after Christ's ascension just as they have in generations since, and will do the same during the last generation before Christ's return (Philippians 3:10-21; Colossians 1:9-29; 4:12; 1 Peter 1:1-25; 2 Peter 1:1-12). Perfection equals functional maturity. Saints of every generation have and do attain to this perfection.

The woman of Revelation 12 is Israel. And the man child is Jesus Christ. The present church (Jew and Gentile) and Israel are dealt with separately, though in parallel, during the church age, with Israel eventually coming back to God (Romans 11:7-37; Revelation 7:1-8) and becoming one with the church.

The bride of Christ is the true church of every generation since Christ's ascension and will include the remnant of Israel that is saved preceding Christ's reign (John 3:28-30; Romans 7:4; 1 Corinthians 12:12-27; 2 Corinthians 11:2; Ephesians 1:15-23; 5:22-32; Revelation 19:7-9; 21:1-5, 9-19).

In summary, it can be seen that the major errors uncovered here extend into the areas of soteriology (study of salvation; in this case specifically the aspect of sanctification), ecclesiology (study of the church), and eschatology (study of the end times). Therefore, it is a serious condition that must be confronted when it is promoted in the church. Many people are blinded and snared because of the subtleties involved together with the lure of elitism. Then, of course, the issues of discerning motives and satanic deception further complicate correction. So, the truth must be spoken firmly, lovingly, and persistently.

More could be written. But for now, this is set forth to promote the process of correction and healing in the body of Christ and to illustrate why foundations of doctrine are necessary.

In retrospect then, doctrine is an essential and currently relevant foundational element. In fact, an examination of the extensive networking taking place today among various apostolic and prophetic ministries reveals that the Holy Spirit is currently desiring to establish a sound doctrinal foundation in His church. He is tempering the body together in this regard.

"But the Helper, the Holy Spirit, whom the Father will send in My name, He will teach you all things, and bring to your remembrance all things that I said to you However, when He, the Spirit of truth, has come, He will guide you into all truth; for He will not speak on His own *authority,* but whatever He hears He will speak; and He will tell you things to come." John 14:26; 16:13

Proper doctrinal foundations will therefore contribute to righteousness in the church, preparing "living stones which are being built up as a spiritual house" (I Peter 2:5). Sound doctrine will always have Christ as the foundation, and in turn, Christ will always be at the center of the building process. Jesus is…and always will be the chief cornerstone and the chief architect and laborer. His methods are not the world's. "But God has chosen the foolish things of the world to put to shame the wise, and God has chosen the weak things of the world to put to shame the things which are mighty" (1 Corinthians 1:27). Later, Paul went on to give the church at Ephesus a revelatory picture of how Christ gets it done. The remainder of this book will reference Ephesians as the apostolic blueprint for building the church. This unfolding mystery calls us all to participate.

Chapter 3

"Heavenly Places and Beyond" Your Position in Christ
Ephesians 1:1-2:7

Who are you and where do you live? The answers to this question come through revelation. In Ephesians chapter one Paul prays, "that the God of our Lord Jesus Christ, the Father of glory, may give to you the spirit of wisdom and revelation in the knowledge of Him" (v.17). We need our eyes opened. "The eyes of your understanding being enlightened; that you may know what is the hope of His calling, what are the riches of the glory of His inheritance in the saints" (v.18).

What takes place when you put your faith in Jesus as the Christ, when you submit to Him as your Lord and

Savior? This is what comprises the foundational stuff of the church. This is at the heart of apostolic and prophetic ministry. Earthly wisdom, common sense, and intellectual advancement are not the required skills for understanding Christ's plans. Revelation is the key...embraced through faith. "**Now faith is the substance of things hoped for, the evidence of things not seen.**" (Hebrews 11:1). Faith alone, or faith only is how Martin Luther conveyed it. Those who put their faith only in Jesus become one with the Chief Cornerstone.

This is what the New Testament church was founded upon. After centuries of darkness the church of the Reformation resumed the process. The rediscovery of the priesthood of all believers and the authority of Scripture led the way in a reexamination of church government, doctrinal purity, and a host of issues that continue to be examined up to this very day. True apostolic and prophetic ministry will always spearhead the building of foundations, starting with faith in Jesus Christ and building thereon, ultimately culminating in the completed church at Christ's return.

Though we know these things, are we willing to perpetuate the process? Do we understand it in the Ephesians 1:17-18 sense? I think not. "**But the natural man does not receive the things of the Spirit of God, for they are foolishness to him; nor can he know *them*, because they are spiritually discerned.**" (1 Corinthians 2:14). That is why Paul's first prayer for the Ephesians was ceaseless (1:16). Ours must be as well. We are in need of continual revelation. Peter's dilemma is upon us (Matthew 16:13-25). One moment he was blessed for his recognition of Jesus as the Christ. The very next he stumbled as Satan's tool for failing to grasp the way of the cross. In the church we often begin by faith. Then our intellect gets in the way. But let us get back to how this applies to who we are and where we live.

When you put your faith in Jesus as the Christ, you are in Christ, hence a new creation. "Therefore, if anyone *is* in Christ, *he is* a new creation; old things have passed away; behold, all things have become new." (2 Corinthians 5:17). Whenever the church's eyes are truly opened to this as was referenced in Ephesians, New Testament results will continue to occur. Ephesians 1 declares who we are in Christ. We are "saints" (v. 1). Yes, we are holy ones. We are set apart for God's use. Perhaps you have been taught that only special people who are dead and have been canonized are saints. This is false. "But of Him you are in Christ Jesus, who became for us wisdom from God—and righteousness and sanctification and redemption—" (1 Corinthians 1:30). Every influence of hell and sinful flesh will try and steal this from you.

There was a season when a brother and I ministered to the homosexual community in our city. At the heart of the homosexual's struggle is his identity. Having believed "the lie", that he was created by God to be homosexual; he is given up unto vile affections (see Romans 1:25-27). But God's word stands true. "And such were some of you. But you were washed, but you were sanctified, but you were justified in the name of the Lord Jesus and by the Spirit of our God." (1 Corinthians 6:11). Only by repentance (a change of mind) and pure faith in Jesus can the homosexual be set free. If he refuses to believe that his sins are forgiven and that he is a new creation, he cannot be saved. This is true with any sin or influence that attacks our identity in Christ. You are a saint. When we accept this…when we believe this…when we walk in this, "Nevertheless the solid foundation of God stands, having this seal: "The Lord knows those who are His," and, "Let everyone who names the name of Christ depart from iniquity." (2 Timothy 2:19). The apostolic church is a church of saints. The success of your walk with Christ and ultimately the success of the church are rooted in your identity as saints. "Rise Up O Saints of God!"

You are also "faithful". Yes that is what v.1 says. It means: because Christ is faithful, you are faithful. You are in the faithful one. He is in you. We not only have faith in The Faithful One, but His faithfulness is in us. When the church stands upon the foundation of faithfulness in Christ…when your eyes are opened to see your faithfulness in Christ, "…the gates of Hades shall not prevail against it." (Matthew 16:18). Are you getting it yet? Are the eyes of your understanding being enlightened? We must believe and walk in the truth of who God declares us to be. If, after believing in Jesus as your Lord and Savior, you still see yourself as unholy or unfaithful, you will miss your purpose in life and the grand role that you play as a member of Christ's church.

Ephesians 1:3 continues to declare your foundational identity in Christ. The phrase "blessed us with every spiritual blessing", used only here in the New Testament, literally means that God has pronounced a eulogy upon us. We use the word eulogy to describe the character and accomplishments of one who is deceased, typically at a funeral. God's eulogy concerning us blesses "us with every spiritual blessing in the heavenly *places* in Christ".

The implications of this are reformational. They move us into who we are in Christ and beyond to where we should be living, literally in "the heavenlies". Two Greek words form this concept. These include a preposition that indicates a superimposition of time, place, and order…and a noun referring to the abode of God. By implication it is a place/time of happiness, power, and eternity. Vine sums it up by saying it is "the place where Christ sits, the present position of believers in relationship to Christ, the present position where we possess every spiritual blessing".[iv] It is here that we are blessed with all spiritual blessings in Christ because it is where Christ now dwells, at God's right hand (1:20).

It is where we are now raised up and made to sit together with Christ Jesus (2:6). This is where the church is presently called to declare the manifold wisdom of God to the principalities and powers (3:10). And this is the field of our warfare against the principalities, powers, rulers of the darkness of this world, and spiritual wickedness (6:12).

Either this is true or it is not true. God says that you are blessed with all spiritual blessings. All means all, not some. His pronouncement or eulogy declares that every thing that is in Christ is to be yours. We are blessed! Before the church can do all that God calls it to, we must accept all that God declares us to be. Before the church can demonstrate the kingdom of God coming in power, we must live where God says we live. We continue to need the eyes of our understanding enlightened. Paul's prayer (1:15-23) must be our prayer. It is our on-going connection with our identity and position in Christ. This is our greatest need as the church… to see who we are and to dwell where Christ dwells. We are in the world. But we are not of this world. Where do you live? You must realize your position in the heavenly places if you are to have heavenly influence upon this earth and beyond.

This does not have to do with our performance but with our position. Man's traditions work against us. The Pharisees displayed an outward appearance that was based on adherence to the law and tradition. Jesus saw right through it. They were not built on the foundation that is in Christ. When the church bases its identity upon performance, we too fall short. When the church bases its success upon adherence to standards, we fail. When a church bases itself upon tradition, structure, accomplishment or comparison to other "less than achieving" churches, a downward spiral of decay begins. Humility demands that we rest in who God says that we are and that we live where God says that we dwell. His life, purpose, and kingdom power can then come forth in our midst.

Peter's ministry to Cornelius's household illustrates these principles. The church did not yet include Gentile converts and was already becoming Pharisaical. Though Peter was blessed in the heavenlies (Ephesians 1:3), he needed his eyes enlightened in order to move on into the harvest and labor with Christ who said He would build His church. So God gave him a vision. Peter **"and saw heaven opened and an object like a great sheet bound at the four corners, descending to him and let down to the earth."** (Acts 10:11). You can follow the story. Against his inclinations he nonetheless ended up in the house of Cornelius. While preaching the gospel, ending with the declaration, **"…whoever believes in Him will receive remission of sins."** (Acts 10:43), the Holy Spirit fell on the Gentiles. The other Jews that were with Peter were astonished. Peter concluded that these Gentiles must also be part of the church because they were baptized with the Holy Spirit. He later used the same argument to convince the other apostles and brothers in Judea that the Gentiles were now called to be part of the church. But in the natural, Peter and all the other Jewish believers not only saw the Gentiles as unclean, but were prone to apply outward standards as a measure of their acceptance before God. They still had much to learn. The Council of Jerusalem (Acts 15) should have established the fact. Even though it was a step in the right direction, the church still attached conditions to the Gentile segment of the church, saying that they needed to abstain from certain things. Time however would show that the Judaizers were not satisfied; hence Paul addresses this subject in his letter to the Galatians.

At least two lessons can be derived from this illustration. When true saving faith responds to the gospel, God declares us holy, faithful, and blessed with all spiritual blessings in heavenly places in Christ. Men, even godly men who have already received these things, are prone to establish external standards for others. This is hypocrisy. We need the eyes of our understanding enlightened.

Today's church, the Assemblies of God included, continues to establish unwarranted standards and structures that limit the grace of God. We must repent and have our eyes opened on an on-going basis.

Common church membership requirements are a case in point. Though there may be reasonable criteria for recognizing fellowship among us, salvation is the only scriptural requirement for church membership. **"For as the body is one and has many members, but all the members of that one body, being many, are one body, so also *is* Christ. For by one Spirit we were all baptized into one body—whether Jews or Greeks, whether slaves or free—and have all been made to drink into one Spirit."** (1 Corinthians 12:12-13).

Does this then rule out all sectarianism and denominationalism? Evidently this is not the case because God has blessed many varieties of these throughout church history. However, sects and denominations that view themselves as the only true Christian church and/or establish extra-scriptural standards are on a slippery slope.

We improperly regulate membership because we misunderstand Divine government (this will be further addressed later). We try and filter membership as a way to manipulate congregational decisions, all the while failing to see that congregational government is not God's plan.

It is the ministry of the apostles and prophets that establishes and maintains the foundational framework of government within the church, including setting the church in order and ordaining elders (Acts 14:23; Titus 1:5). Concerning the foundation, the apostle insists on nothing more and nothing less. He preaches the kingdom of God, not shunning to declare all of God's counsel (Acts 20:25,27). Though it is not the intent of this writing to expound on the role of prophet, suffice it to say that the prophet has the testimony of Jesus, which is the spirit of prophecy (Revelation 19:10). The prophet speaks unto men to edification, and exhortation, and comfort (1 Corinthians 14:3), often forth telling, sometimes foretelling. As Dennis Cramer words it, the prophet speaks to the potential of the church. Because of these unique roles, the church not only chaffs in response to apostles and prophets but often rejects their ministries out of hand.

Ephesians includes much more concerning who we are and where we dwell. Consider the aspects of our calling… past, present, and future. God "…chose us in Him before the foundation of the world, that we should be holy and without blame before Him in love" (1:4). This speaks to our order in God's creative genius.

Before Satan fell from heaven to the earth, God knew what role the church would play in destroying the enemy's works and bringing the gospel of the kingdom to all the world. Before Adam and Eve fell in the garden God "…predestined us to adoption as sons by Jesus Christ to Himself, according to the good pleasure of His will" (1:5). As already discussed, we are presently blessed with all spiritual blessings in heavenly places in Christ. Bill Johnson's When Heaven Invades Earth is a wonderful contemporary application of how the church's message and methods should converge to bring heavenly results on earth. Apostolic anointing calls the church to nothing less than a present demonstration of Holy Spirit power declaring the gospel of Christ's kingdom.

"And I, brethren, when I came to you, did not come with excellence of speech or of wisdom declaring to you the testimony of God. For I determined not to know anything among you except Jesus Christ and Him crucified. I was with you in weakness, in fear, and in much trembling. And my speech and my preaching *were* not with persuasive words of human wisdom, but in demonstration of the Spirit and of power, that your faith should not be in the wisdom of men but in the power of God." (1 Corinthians 2:1-5).

The Ephesians needed "...the eyes of your (their) understanding ... enlightened; that you (they) may know what is the hope of His calling, what are the riches of the glory of His inheritance in the saints" (1:18). We too must have the eyes of our understanding enlightened to these things through prayer, that we may know the hope of our calling. Verse 19 goes on to specify that this includes knowing "...what *is* the exceeding greatness of His power toward us who believe, according to the working of His mighty power". It is the apostolic anointing that settles only for a "signs following" confirmation of the gospel. Paul's declaration in 2 Corinthians 12:12 affirms this. "Truly the signs of an apostle were accomplished among you with all perseverance, in signs and wonders and mighty deeds." His testimony to the Romans does the same.

"For I will not dare to speak of any of those things which Christ has not accomplished through me, in word and deed, to make the Gentiles obedient—

in mighty signs and wonders, by the power of the Spirit of God, so that from Jerusalem and round about to Illyricum I have fully preached the gospel of Christ." (Romans 15:18-19).

Even though the power of the Holy Spirit and all His manifestations are to be sought and administered by the whole body (Stephen and Philip are wonderful examples of this), it is the apostolic pattern that insists that this full gospel includes signs and wonders (see Acts 4:29-33). But much of the church today denies these realities.

Again, from Ephesians, this includes a <u>present</u> sealing of God's Holy Spirit of promise (1:13-14). The apostolic anointing insists as well that the church experiences the same baptism of the Holy Spirit that occurred on the day of Pentecost. Paul's reference to this must be understood in connection with his ministry to them as recorded in Acts 19:1-6. After asking them, "Did you receive the Holy Spirit when you believed?" he proceeded to lay hands on them with Pentecostal results. Peter also ministered the same Pentecostal sealing to Cornelius's household (Acts 10) and later (Acts 11) defended his experience with them by telling the apostles and brethren in Jerusalem,

"And as I began to speak, the Holy Spirit fell upon them, as upon us at the beginning. Then I remembered the word of the Lord, how He said, 'John indeed baptized with water, but you shall be baptized with the Holy Spirit.' If therefore God gave them the same gift as *He gave* us when we believed on the Lord Jesus Christ, who was I that I could withstand God?"

This "earnest of our inheritance", the baptism in the Holy Spirit, is intended to signify that there is a greater dimension to our inheritance now and in the future. We have not only "obtained our inheritance" (1:11), but can also

"...know what is the hope of His calling, what are the riches of the glory of His inheritance in the saints, and what *is* the exceeding greatness of His power toward us who believe, according to the working of His mighty power which He worked in Christ when He raised Him from the dead and seated *Him* at His right hand in the heavenly *places*" (Ephesians 1:18-20).

In other words the apostolic pattern is to call the church to a present Pentecostal experience that demonstrates the resurrection power of Christ. Within the Assemblies of God, what was originally our Pentecostal distinctive has again and again been compromised. We must again accept our mandate to see this Pentecostal blessing spread throughout the whole church, not set it aside in interdenominational discussions as we are prone to do.

Today there is a very strong denial of Holy Spirit manifestation and resurrection power in the church. And I am not just referring to the cessationists and dispensationalists.

There is great resistance in Pentecostal and Charismatic circles as well. Assembly of God congregations are being split down the middle on the pretext that lying signs and wonders must be avoided. While this is a prophetic warning given to the Thessalonians (2 Thessalonians 2:1-12), context connects these lying wonders to the son of perdition, the defilement of the Jewish temple, the absence of the Holy Spirit in the church, Satanic enablement, rejection of the truth, and pleasure in unrighteousness.

The problem in the church is that the saints need enlightenment. If the eyes of our understanding are not enlightened we will end up like the Jews, who witnessed all the miracles of Jesus but rejected Him as the Christ. If the eyes of our understanding are not enlightened, we will find ourselves on that slippery slope of last days peril, "having a form of godliness but denying its power. And from such people turn away!" (2 Timothy 3: 5).

We must see God's Holy Spirit power as the present earnest of our inheritance. God's solution is to provide anointed apostolic ministry that demonstrates an authentic "signs and wonders" confirmation of the gospel. Note the way Paul uses the term Christ when connecting the experience of the church to the power of the Holy Spirit. **Christ is the designation of Jesus as the anointed one.** The church is designed to operate in nothing less than this anointing.

"That He would grant you, according to the riches of His glory, to be strengthened with might through His Spirit in the inner man, that **Christ** may dwell in your hearts through faith; that you, being rooted and grounded in love, may be able to comprehend with all the saints what *is* the width and length and depth and height—to know the love of **Christ** which passes knowledge; that you may be filled with all the fullness of God. Now to Him who is able to do exceedingly abundantly above all that we ask or think, according to the power that works in us, to Him *be* glory in the church by **Christ** Jesus to all generations, forever and ever. Amen." (Ephesians 3:16-21, emphasis mine).

This power that Jesus said would accompany those who believe on him (Acts 1:8) is also connected with our relationship to the Father through Jesus.

"Most assuredly, I say to you, he who believes in Me, the works that I do he will do also; and greater *works* than these he will do, because I go to My Father. And whatever you ask in My name, that I will do, that the Father may be glorified in the Son. If you ask anything in My name, I will do *it*." (John 14:12-14).

I am sure that it is obvious by now to all who are reading this that I am a Pentecostal. 2006 recorded the 100th anniversary of the Azusa Street Revival. As we know, that was one of several locations where the Holy Spirit fell on hungry believers, affecting the church worldwide even to this day. At first many who experienced Pentecost were alienated from their traditional Christian churches. As decades passed the Pentecostals moved from notoriety to respectability. The "Latter Rain Movement" caused a stir and many in it were in turn alienated from "mainline" Pentecostals. The "Charismatic Renewal" brought a denominational breadth to Pentecostal phenomena that even the Pentecostals marveled at.

From my relatively short almost forty year exposure to these trends in the church, I now see an alarming pattern developing. There appears to be a more pronounced backlash to Pentecost springing up. Yes, there continues to be the same resistance by the cessationists and dispensationalists referred to earlier. But within Pentecostal and Charismatic circles there is outright skepticism to the validity of events surrounding Toronto, Pensacola, and beyond. It is refreshing to visit historical and/or contemporary reformations and revivals and see again and again that God's sovereignty is repeatedly at the source of this activity. Wherever men yield to God in humility and prayer, recognizing their inability to save a soul, heal the sick, raise the dead, or live a holy life…wherever men turn from their wicked and pride-filled ways…wherever men call out to God in desperation for that same experience testified by the book of Acts, Jesus has a way of sovereignly drawing near, and revealing himself. Our greatest need is a continual thirst for an increased outpouring of the Holy Spirit in the church. It is very clear that the admonition to the church in Ephesus at the end of the first Century (Revelation 2:1-5) is most applicable to us today as well. We must return to our "first love" and "first works" or our candlestick will be removed.

The text of Ephesians continues with the thought of our position in Christ. We are now adopted as sons (Ephesians 1:5); but not as earthly parents adopt. We are literally born again as God's children (1 Peter 1:3) by the same seed of the Holy Spirit who conceived Jesus. God does not adopt believers as children. Rather they are begotten as such by His Holy Spirit through faith. And since we have received the adoption of sons, God desires to send forth the Spirit of his Son into our hearts crying, "Abba, Father!" proving that we are heirs (Galatians 4:5-7). This was so crucial to Paul's understanding of our identity that he connected the reception of the Holy Spirit by faith and the working of miracles by the hearing of faith to our inclusion as children of Abraham.

> "O foolish Galatians! Who has bewitched you that you should not obey the truth before whose eyes Jesus Christ was clearly portrayed among you as crucified? This only I want to learn from you: Did you receive the Spirit by the works of the law, or by the hearing of faith? Are you so foolish? Having begun in the Spirit, are you now being made perfect by the flesh? Have you suffered so many things in vain—if indeed *it was* in vain?
> Therefore He who supplies the Spirit to you and works miracles among you, *does He do it* by the works of the law, or by the hearing of faith?— just as Abraham *"believed God, and it was accounted to him for righteousness."* Therefore know

that *only* those who are of faith are sons of Abraham." (Galatians 3:1-7).

As children (sons) we also have now received an inheritance (Ephesians 1:11). Vine again gives us insight into this term by defining it as "...the condition and possession of the believer in the new order of things to be ushered in at the return of Christ".[v] Beyond what was mentioned earlier concerning the "earnest of our inheritance", let me again reiterate that much of our inheritance is presently going unrecognized and unused because the eyes of our understanding need further enlightenment. In the next section (Ephesians 2:8-3:21) more will be said about this in connection with the word "now". But let us consider one more reference that defines our position in Christ. That is our predestination (Ephesians 1:5, 11).

Traditional understanding often limits this term to the nature of our salvation, explaining it as limiting in advance and/or determining before. Verse 5 connects it with "adoption" and "the good pleasure of his will". We've already considered some of the implications concerning adoption. Verse 11 also connects predestination with His purpose and work, and again "the counsel of his own will". Who we are and where we live surely are affected by our understanding of this concept. Romans 8:29, in context, makes it clear that the primary focus of God's will is first who we are. "For whom He foreknew, He also predestined *to be* conformed to the image of His Son, that He might be the firstborn among many brethren." From the perspective of love, 1 John 4:17(c) declares, "...because as He is, so are we in this world". God has predestined us to be like Jesus. He has predestinated us to be saints, faithful, adopted sons, given an inheritance, blessed with all spiritual blessings in heavenly places in Christ. We are now prepared to see how grace and the church bring us to heavenly places and beyond.

Chapter 4

"Heavenly Places and Beyond" Grace and the Church
Ephesians 2:8-3:21

Declaring who we are (saints, faithful, blessed, adopted, heirs, predestined) and where we live (heavenly places) is the jumping off point for grace, through which this glorious church of which we are part owes its existence. As we continually pray in light of Ephesians 1:15-23, our humble petition solicits that heavenly supply of the desire and power to do God's will. James 4:6 and 1 Peter 5:5 echo the tie between humility and grace (God gives grace to the humble). Philippians 2:13 defines grace without mentioning the term, "For it is God who works in you both to will and to do for *His* good pleasure". Paul told the Corinthians that he "labored more abundantly than they all, yet not I, but the grace of God *which was with me.*" (1 Corinthians 15:10). Grace links our past (Ephesians 1:2-6) to the present (1:7; 2:5-8) and gives us power to minister now and in the future (3:2,7,8). According to Vine, in its noun form grace depicts graciousness, divine influence, benefit, and gift; as a verb, to cheer, be well, glad, God speed, rejoice.[vi] It is no wonder that it is used so abundantly as both a salutation and closing in this and other New Testament letters. According to Ephesians 4:7 and Romans 12:6 it is the "measure" of grace that determines the scope and nature of Christ's ministry through us.

We are often pre-occupied with the past or the future. Ephesians gives us several words of instruction that help explain how grace works through the individual and in turn produces the corporate influence of the church. The first is that we are His workmanship (3:10). Through grace we are "created in Christ Jesus for good works". God has "prepared beforehand that we should walk in them." When Jesus said that He would build His church and the gates of hell would not prevail against it (Matthew 16:18), He certainly knew that He would be commissioning his disciples (us) to bring the gospel of the kingdom to the whole world...He working in us and through us (Matthew 28:18-20). Grace enables us to understand and function in the role Christ designed for us. This is the "dispensation" of grace that Paul refers to in Ephesians 3:2 (see also 1 Corinthians 9:17 and Colossians 1:25). And it is with this understanding that Christ sets apart what is referred to as the five-fold ministry for the perfecting of the saints as a whole (Ephesians 4:7-16). More will be said about this in the following section.

The second word of instruction to help us at this juncture is "remember" (Ephesians 2:11). Both here and in Ephesians 2:2-3 our former life apart from Christ is given sharp contrast to our present position. There is no place for a fleshly past in this present endeavor. In John 15:1-16 Jesus teaches that we cannot bear fruit of ourselves. We can only bear fruit if we abide in Him and His words abide in us. The Father is glorified as we bear much fruit. We are chosen and ordained to bring forth fruit that remains. His church produces lasting fruit through the influence of grace.

This brings us to the third word, "now". In the emphatic form it could be rendered "just now, the present, immediate, this time". Used in Ephesians 2:13; 3:5, 10; and 5:8 it is NOW that we are in Christ, NOW that the mystery of the church is revealed, NOW that the manifold wisdom of God is known, and NOW that we are light.

It seems that we are prone to wait for things to happen. Here we are reminded that there is no time like the present to be the church. We must not let the devil rob us. We must not let our wills deny us. We must not let circumstances deceive us or discourage us. Paul's instruction to the elders at Ephesus complements this discussion of grace and our work at this time. "So now, brethren, I commend you to God and to the word of His grace, which is able to build you up and give you an inheritance among all those who are sanctified." (Acts 20:32).

Grace is what fuels the church. In Ephesians 2 the church is referred to as "one body" (v. 16), "the household of God" (v. 19), "an holy temple" (v. 21), "an habitation of God" (v. 22). As the church we are God's utensil, vehicle, means, and method of revealing the gospel of the kingdom. God "...put all *things* under His feet, and gave Him *to be* head over all *things* to the church" (Ephesians 1:22); "To the intent that now the manifold wisdom of God might be made known by the church to the principalities and powers in the heavenly *places*" (Ephesians 3:10); that "to Him *be* glory in the church by Christ Jesus to all generations, forever and ever. Amen" (Ephesians 3:21). To my knowledge there is not a place in Scripture that refers to a material building as the church. Hence all of this refers to what God intends to do in us and through us, His people.

Paul's second prayer in this epistle (3:14-19) goes beyond the enlightenment of Christ's power prayed for earlier to actual empowerment,

"to be strengthened with might through His Spirit in the inner man, that Christ may dwell in your hearts through faith; that you, being rooted and grounded in love, may be able to comprehend with all the saints what *is* the width and length and depth and height—to know the love of Christ which passes knowledge; that you may be filled with all the fullnessofGod. "

This prayer leads to one of the most remarkable proclamations in all of Scripture. The question is: Will we the church accept who God says that we are and live where He says that we live? If so, He "…is able to do exceedingly abundantly above all that we ask or think, according to the power that works in us, to Him *be* glory in the church by Christ Jesus to all generations, forever and ever. Amen." Ephesians 3:20-21. Will you walk in your calling?

Chapter 5

"Heavenly Places and Beyond" Walking In Your Calling
Ephesians 4:1-7

Well, I don't feel like a saint, I am not always faithful. Are you sure that I am predestined to an inheritance as an adopted son? The serpent's conversation with Eve hasn't changed much has it? "Has God said?" Saints of God, we have an on-going choice to make. We have already been introduced to God's method for realizing our identity and living where we belong. It is by walking in the works already prepared (2:10). These are the "greater works" Jesus referenced in John 14:12.

We are now called to look further at what it means to walk. Simply stated, it is putting one foot in front of the other. Isaiah had a prophetic glimpse when he wrote, "Your ears shall hear a word behind you, saying, 'This *is* the way, walk in it', whenever you turn to the right hand or whenever you turn to the left." Isaiah 30:21. Will we listen for that voice so that we may identify the prepared works?

What parent doesn't bubble over with joy when his/her baby takes its first step? How sad it is if that child fails to progress with other steps, or worse yet, if that first step is never taken. Our Father is yearning for us to walk. Our Father has prepared the way. Jesus has walked the road. The Holy Spirit is in us to guide us. We must put one foot in front of the other. The church is not called to do it all at once. Jesus taught us the value of living each day in God's grace. No Christian is called to do it alone. We are a body. So, let us walk worthy (4:1). As the eyes of our understanding are enlightened to the hope of our calling (1:18), let us walk worthy. Our vocation (calling) is both high (Philippians 3:14) and holy (2 Timothy1:9). We are "…partakers of the heavenly calling" Hebrews 3:1. We are the very expression of God's kingdom on earth. That is why we are to walk worthy, "With all lowliness and gentleness, with longsuffering, bearing with one another in love, endeavoring to keep the unity of the Spirit in the bond of peace." (4:2-3).

Just as the will of God first deals with the formation of Christ in us, so our walk must be focused on character and relationship among us. This chapter of Ephesians unites our calling with our corporate function. Before we look further at walking, we would do well to examine three aspects of our function as a body.

Already referenced is unity (v.3). This is the unity of the Spirit. This is not the arbitrary agreement of men. When Jesus spoke of it in John 17, He prayed "that they may be one as We *are*." (v.11) and "that they all may be one, as You, Father, *are* in Me, and I in You; that they also may be one in Us, that the world may believe that You sent Me." (v.21). Religious ecumenism is largely based on man's desire to get along at the expense of God's word. True unity is found only in the agreement of the Father and the Son. It is the unity of the Spirit. We must submit to it and keep it in the bond of peace.

A second aspect of our corporate function is diversity (v.7). Though this word is not used, it is certainly described. There is one body, one Spirit, one hope, one Lord, one faith, one baptism, one God and Father. But, there is a diverse membership. Every member is given grace according to measure. According to 1 Corinthians 12, "But now God has set the members, each one of them, in the body just as He pleased." (v.18), "…But God composed the body, having given greater honor to that *part* which lacks it …" (v.24), "that there should be no schism in the body …" (v.25).

However, for the most part, the church has become largely a body of spectators. The ministers and the ministry have become stereotyped. Concerning the body, it is God's intent that every member be involved in ministry. Again in Ephesians 4, the ministry gifts (v. 11) have been given "for the equipping of the saints for the work of ministry, for the edifying of the body of Christ" (v. 12), "from whom the whole body, joined and knit together by what every joint supplies, according to the effective working by which every part does its share, causes growth of the body for the edifying of itself in love" (v.16).

For this to take place, the earlier mentioned stereotyped ministry must return to the biblical foundation. Only then can the third aspect of our corporate function be realized. That would be maturity (v. 13). "Till we all come to the unity of the faith and of the knowledge of the Son of

God, to a perfect man, to the measure of the stature of the fullness of Christ". The anointing Jesus referred to in Luke 4:18 should also be upon us. Preaching the gospel, healing the sick, even raising the dead are Christ's plan and purpose for every believer. In order to come to maturity, a full operating ministry needs to be functioning. Hopefully the learning curve of our history will illustrate the process and give us a greater hunger to press on to maturity. But first, a more complete look at church government including and beyond Ephesians is necessary. Then reflection again upon our personal story may give you insight about how to proceed where you are.

Chapter 6

"Heavenly Places and Beyond" Government is Divine
Ephesians 4:8-16

Simple observation will reveal that there are three major types of church government in operation today. They are Episcopal, Presbyterian and Congregational. It could be argued that each of these has its advantages. However, none of them are truly foundational for they all revolve around men. Remember, man has a tremendous capacity to build apart from God.

Episcopal government is in essence where bishops govern the church through relationship based on heirarchy. The Roman Catholic Church best exemplifies such government with the Pope being the head bishop. Practically speaking, human authority is the ultimate issue and of course ends in human fallibility, contrary to the whole system proposed by the Catholics. But other groups not claiming an infallible human head experience the same result because on every level a man is seen as the residing governmental voice. In our movement we would view this as dictatorial influence when a man insists on his own way. Yet it affects us at all levels when strong leadership exceeds its God-given role.

Presbyterian government attempts to diffuse the influence of one man by adhering to plurality. That is, groups of men convene in councils or "presbyteries". These groups are typically made up of ordained clergy and/or representative elders from congregations. Though closer to the New Testament model, plurality too breaks down when the authority of men is made the focus. This tension is displayed when presbyteries issue decisions or policies that may extend beyond God-given prerogatives. In the Assemblies of God Presbyterian government has been typically practiced on the District and General Council levels, although it is increasing among the local churches.

Congregational government is grass roots democracy incorporated into the church. Every man has a vote and the majority rules. This type of government is particularly popular in the United States and other places where a democratic/republic form of secular government is present. And, typically, this form of government is at work in local churches of the Assemblies of God. However, God has not revealed government for the people and by the people as His model for the church. Even though there are examples of democracy in the New Testament (the nomination of deacons in Acts 6:3, "Therefore, brethren, seek out from among you seven men of *good* reputation, full of the Holy Spirit and wisdom, whom we may appoint over this business" and the affirmation of apostolic/elder policy in Acts 15:22, "Then it pleased the apostles and elders, with the whole church, to send chosen men of their own company ...", congregational rule is not ordained by God. In the Assemblies of God, it has been my observation that confusion and instability can occur when democratic influence extend beyond the limited use illustrated in New Testament practice. In fact, many Assemblies of God churches continually face "power struggles" because strong voices in the congregations are trying to lead while pastors are likewise trying to lead. Or elected boards are in a similar way trying to give direction to the pastor, and hence the church. A more crucial example is in the congregational <u>selection</u> of ministers and the <u>origin</u> of church policy. As will be noted below, generally speaking, decision making that affects the church should be rooted in an understanding of Theocracy. Though the Assemblies of God has incorporated a hybrid of presbyterian and congregational New Testament examples into its governmental structure, we need a further revelation of a more complete Biblical form of government.

These brief definitions of church government may serve to clarify biblical government that is truly foundational. But what is government? At the root it has to do with authority. It has to do with power. It has to do with God.

Among the revealed names of God, two should be observed here, El Shaddai and Adonai Jehovah. El Shaddai is commonly understood to mean Almighty God. Scofield more clearly describes Shaddai as "All-sufficient" with El already expressing "Almightiness". Hence, together they form "Almighty All-sufficient". This is God. This is authority. This is power. That was God's revelation to Abraham in Genesis 17:1 "When Abram was ninety-nine years old, the LORD appeared to Abram and said to him, "I *am* Almighty God; walk before Me and be blameless."

Yet God also reveals Himself as Adonai Jehovah. Here, Adonai is understood as "Master" and Jehovah as "The

Self-existent One". "But Abram said, "Lord GOD (Adonai Jehovah), what will You give me, seeing I go childless, and the heir of my house *is* Eliezer of Damascus?"" Genesis 15:2. Suffice it to say that God is the ultimate in power, authority...and government. With this in mind, Isaiah 9:6,7 significantly relates to the developing thesis.

> "For unto us a Child is born, Unto us a Son is given; And the government will be upon His shoulder. And His name will be called Wonderful, Counselor, Mighty God, Everlasting Father, Prince of Peace. Of the increase of *His* government and peace *there will be* no end, Upon the throne of David and over His kingdom, To order it and establish it with judgment and justice From that time forward, even forever.
> The zeal of the Lord of hosts will perform this."

In a congruent manner, the angel said unto Mary in Luke 1:31-33,

> "And behold, you will conceive in your womb and bring forth a Son, and shall call His name JESUS. He will be great, and will be called the Son of the

Highest; and the Lord God will give Him the throne of His father David. And He will reign over the house of Jacob forever, and of His kingdom there will be no end."

Paul crystallizes the progression of thought in Ephesians 1:19-23,

"And what *is* the exceeding greatness of His power toward us who believe, according to the working of His mighty power which He worked in Christ when He raised Him from the dead and seated *Him* at His right hand in the heavenly *places,* far above all principality and power and might and dominion, and every name that is named, not only in this age but also in that which is to come. And He put all *things* under His feet, and gave Him *to be* head over all *things* to the church, which is His body, the fullness of Him who fills all in all."

Foundational church government is rooted in the person Jesus Christ. There is no other government in His church. If Israel's government under Moses was a theocracy, then the church's government can be nothing less. But how can such a thing be? Jesus Himself described the process.

"...All authority has been given to Me in heaven and on earth. Go therefore and make disciples of all the nations, baptizing them in the name of the Father and of the Son and of the Holy Spirit, teaching them to observe all things that I have commanded you; and lo, I am with you always, *even* to the end of the age." Amen." Matthew 28:18-20

There can only be one head in the church. " And He is the head of the body, the church, who is the beginning, the firstborn from the dead, that in all things He may have the preeminence." Colossians 1:18. All men must defer to the head for foundational government to exist. Man's role must be purely functional.

Now granted, each of the three forms of church government previously described may in voice adhere to this truth, saying that Christ can rule through these structures. But experience contradicts the claim. Even though it is difficult (and possibly a mistake) to try and fix a name upon this pattern, the following scriptures are presented here to illustrate that we truly can allow Christ to rule in His church through what could be called "Functional Church Government".

"Therefore He says: "*When He ascended on high, He led captivity captive, And gave gifts to men.*"(Now this, *"He ascended"* — what does it mean but that He also first descended into the lower parts of the earth? He who descended is also the One who ascended far above all the heavens, that He might fill all things.)And He Himself gave some *to be* apostles, some prophets, some evangelists, and some pastors and teachers, for the equipping of the saints for the work of ministry, for the edifying of the body of Christ, till we all come to the unity of the faith and of the knowledge of the Son of God, to a perfect man, to the measure of the stature of the fullness of Christ." Ephesians 4:8-13

"For this reason I left you in Crete, that you should set in order the things that are lacking, and appoint elders in every city as I commanded you." Titus 1:5

"The elders who are among you I exhort, I who am a fellow elder and a witness of the sufferings of Christ, and also a partaker of the glory that will be revealed: Shepherd the flock of God which is among you, serving as overseers, not by compulsion but willingly, not for dishonest gain but eagerly; nor as being lords over those entrusted to you, but being examples to the flock;

and when the Chief Shepherd appears, you will receive the crown of glory that does not fade away." I Peter 5:1-4

The pattern in these verses reveals the following. Christ chooses men and gives them to His church as functioning agents of His headship. These men are (and only can be) functional in their roles of implementing Christ's rule. A brief description of each of these gifts will add further light.

Apostles are literally "those sent forth". Their function is to spearhead the gospel where there is yet no church and correspondingly lay down absolute foundations for it, the emphasis being the latter. For instance, the gospel can reach an area through a variety of means, a church consequently born, and yet foundations are needed. Acts 8:4-17 describes the ministry of Philip (an evangelist) and the subsequent function of Peter and John (apostles) to illustrate this. The complementing ministries of Apollos and Paul illustrate this as well in Acts 18:24-19:7 and in 1 Corinthians 3:5-7. Authority is vested in the anointing that is upon or within the functioning agent. It is extended through loving service, much as God intended in marriage, which will be discussed later.

The prophetic ministry is that which "speaks forth or openly". The prophet's function is to express God's heart concerning the Divine counsels of grace while both forth-telling and fore-telling the purposes of God. Both Old and New Testament prophets often faced rejection because of the intensity and impact of their message. The church today also often struggles in response to God's prophets, especially when their not given within the parameters of edification, exhortation, and comfort. It could be said that the influence of such ministry is directional in nature. As previously pointed out, prophets are included with the apostles as foundational ministries. The book of Acts pictures prophets predicting events to come (13:1-ff), and confirming direction and details of Divine leading (15:30-33; 20:22-23; 21:10-14). Prophets were included both at Jerusalem and Antioch among the active ministers in the early life of the church.

Evangelists are "messengers of good news" or "those who proclaim the Gospel". Philip demonstrated this function and acquired the name of such (Acts 6:26-40; 21:8). The preaching of the Gospel message to the unsaved and subsequently the expansion of the church through new conversions is obviously the functional result of evangelistic ministry.

Pastors are literally shepherds who tend flocks. Referred to directly only in Ephesians 4:11, the function parallels that of elders in Acts 20:28-32 and I Peter 5:2-4, where feeding, leading, and protecting of the flock are the main objectives. This is the most prevalent ministry gift. And for this reason, pastor has unfortunately become the "default" descriptive title for ministers today. Consequently, a functionally diverse ministry has generally not been recognized. Terms like "pastoral staff" have replaced scriptural terms, again limiting the diversity that God has designed for the church.

Teachers have the purest functional title. Jesus is directly referred to as a teacher in John 3:2. Interestingly, a direct warning is given to not take lightly this responsibility (James 3:1). Like prophets they were a designated body in Acts 13:1. Clearly, a teacher is one who delivers and expounds the Word of God. These ministers also deserve a more functionally distinct role in the church.

Before we move on there are some additional thoughts about church planting and the apostolic role that are fitting here especially since this work is written from an apostolic perspective.

It has been a common thought within our movement to equate the term "church planter" with apostle. This is done to avoid the controversy that inevitably arises about the validity of modern apostles. Also, the term "missionary" is often seen as the modern derivative of the apostolic gift. Again, this may be to soften the implications of embracing modern day apostles and preserve our existing governmental structures. But we are complicating the issue. Is the apostle's role primarily to start new churches? No. The apostles were those sent with a message. Sometimes this was a message to the unchurched (Acts 2:14), but more often to the church (Acts 8:1,14; 9:31,32). Christ, in His sovereignty builds the church (Matthew 16:18), adds to the church (Acts 2:47), deletes from the church (Acts 5:1-11), sets the members in the church as it pleases Him (1 Corinthians 3:6-7; 12:18), gifts the members accordingly (Romans 12:3-16; Ephesians 4:7-16)…and ultimately determines if any given local church will cease to exist (Revelation 2:5).

Apostles are sent forth with a message. This begins with the foundations outlined in Hebrews 6:1-2, but in its entirety comprises the apostles' doctrine (Acts 2:42). The New Testament consistently illustrates the functional role of apostles (and the other ministry gifts) at virtually every stage of the church's development. Whether it was their ability to explain what was happening on the day of Pentecost, impart the Holy Spirit through the laying on of hands in Samaria or Ephesus, bringing the gospel into unreached regions (e.g., Peter, James, and John to the Jews or Paul and Barnabus to the Gentiles), establishing governmental order (Paul in Lystra, Iconium, Antioch or Ephesus), delegating the same to Timothy or Titus, or writing epistles to the church on any number of subjects…apostles functioned by laying or reestablishing foundations. There was a breadth of maturity and anointing that was up to the task.

Church planting today has become a ministry generally relegated to young ministers who are trying to apply a blueprint of an existing church form. When success is achieved (typically indicated by numbers and a building), this model or form is set forth as the reason for success. In turn this blueprint is tried in other places. In reality the model may be only part of the reason for the success as defined.

Two questions arise. What should be the definition of success? Whom or what are the reasons for success not taking place? Broadly speaking, the first is easier to answer. Success should be defined as the church extended into new regions, previously unreached peoples coming to Christ, demonstrating New Testament characteristics and reproducing the same as they mature. The answer to the second question is at the heart of this chapter and forms much of the rational for this book. Answering it will give much insight into why every individual expression of the church on earth has eventually met with decline. Attempting to answer it has the potential for bringing us closer to what Ephesians 4:13-16 ultimately promises. This is at the heart of the apostolic mandate. The answer to this second question in the context of this writing comes down to this. When the church does not embrace it's apostles and other ministry gifts in their due order/function, success as defined will not occur, because the ascension gifts represent the headship of Christ. This is why those who speak in terms of the church being restored to New Testament patterns from the Reformation to this day see the ascension gifts as the last phase of restoration, Christ again honored as Head.

Uniquely, the five ministry gifts just described are labeled by Paul as "for the equipping of the saints" in Ephesians 4:12. Literally and contextually this means that these ministers "mend" the brokenness that is found in the lives of the saints that they in turn might mutually build one another up into the perfect stature of Christ. Together, the five fold ministry are to represent the headship of Christ. Constituting the eldership of the church both locally and extra-locally they serve as under shepherds to the Chief

Shepherd. Governmentally, they are functional extensions of Jesus...who alone is Head of the body, the church.

We must now look further at the term elder. Elders, by definition, are "older men", either strictly by age or by spiritual maturity, context depending. In the context of functional government as herein described, they are overseers of the church (Acts 20:17,28 and I Peter 5:2). The term presbyter, referred to in these verses, indicates the maturity of their spiritual experience. The term bishop as used in I Timothy 3:1 refers to the nature of their work. As will be discussed below there is an overlapping effect between the five-fold ministry and the office of elder.

From these definitions, church government from a functional perspective can best be understood when these gifts are seen complementing one another through relationship. Christ's government will be in effect when these varied ministries are allowed to function both locally and extra-locally (the strength of relationship ultimately determining the extent and effect of Christ's rule).

"Who then is Paul, and who *is* Apollos, but ministers through whom you believed, as the Lord gave to each one? I planted, Apollos watered, but God gave the increase. So then neither he who plants is anything, nor he who waters, but God who gives the increase. Now he who plants and he who waters are one, and each one will receive his own reward according to his own labor. For we are God's fellow workers; you are

God's field, *you are* God's building."
I Corinthians 3:5-9

"Abide in Me, and I in you. As the branch cannot bear fruit of itself, unless it abides in the vine, neither can you, unless you abide in Me."I am the vine, you *are* the branches. He who abides in Me, and I in him, bears much fruit; for without Me you can do nothing." John 15:4-5.

A few things must be said concerning local and extra-local interaction. Elders are typically seen to function on a local basis. "So when they had appointed elders in every church, and prayed with fasting, they commended them to the Lord in whom they had believed." Acts 14:23.

However, elders can affect a larger sphere of influence as was demonstrated through the edict generated at the council of Jerusalem (Acts 15). In that setting they acted with the apostles to establish a common statement affecting both the Jerusalem church and the Gentiles in Antioch, Syria, and Cilicia. But strength of relationship allowed this to happen. On the other hand, the five fold ministry of Ephesians 4:11 function either locally or extra-locally.

As just illustrated through Acts 14:23, Paul and Barnabas traveled to different cities and churches ministering. Yet Paul and his companions spent longer periods in certain churches such as Antioch (Acts 14:26) and Corinth (Acts 18:11). As already described, elders function predominantly in a pastoral fashion locally. That is why ministers have most commonly come to be referred to as pastors. However, because apostles, prophets, evangelists, and teachers are also referenced as functioning in local churches, they too should be considered elders (Peter calls himself an elder in 1 Peter 5:1). The five Ephesian 4:11 ministries are inherently elders extra-locally, and locally as relationship dictates (Acts 20:17-32; 21:17-18; I Peter 5:1).

Therefore, especially because recognition of the other ministry gifts has diminished, extra effort is needed to identify and make room for them. As will be later illustrated by our own example, most local churches within the Assemblies of God will struggle with this application because of existing pastor and deacon board structures. The problem is compounded because of our limited process of identifying, training, and credentialing ministers. However, a careful and relational process can address this situation. As a result, additional five fold ministers will be inevitably identified from among those who have the unbiblical title of "lay minister". Some deacons will also be more clearly seen as elders. Local churches will be strained to train and equip these newly identified elders and ministers. But local discipleship combined with Berean-type schooling can facilitate this process. The recent trend within our movement that recognizes the sovereignty of the local church to ordain local elders and ministers is a step in this direction. A new "understanding" and cooperation between our bible colleges, Districts, and General Councils will have to develop in order to deal with credentialing issues. Because this effort has generally not been made, we have missed out on the unique grace that Christ intended for the church or an exaggerated demonstration of these gifts has occurred. The result can be a further misunderstanding and even mistrust of the fivefold ministry.

If understood properly, hierarchy should not be an issue with functional church government. Deferring to another's functional gifting in accordance with the needs of the body is the goal. It can be observed that even when five fold ministry is identified and a plurality of elders is in place, ambition or a desire to have the pre-eminence will corrupt functional government. Loving, humble relationships will ultimately defer to the will and authority of Christ.

Paul described the nature of church government from a functional basis as revealed in the following quotes.

"Now these things, brethren, I have figuratively transferred to myself and Apollos for your sakes, that you may learn in us not to think beyond what is written, that none of you may be puffed up on behalf of one against the other. For who makes you differ *from another?* And what do you have that you did not receive? Now if you did indeed receive *it,* why do you boast as if you had not received *it?* You are already full! You are already rich! You have reigned as kings without us—and indeed I could wish you did reign, that we also might reign with you! For I think that God has displayed us, the apostles, last, as men condemned to death; for we have been made a spectacle to the world, both to angels and to men" I Corinthians 4:6-9.

"Then after fourteen years I went up again to Jerusalem with Barnabas, and also took Titus with *me*. And I went up by revelation, and communicated to them that gospel which I preach among the Gentiles, but privately to those who were of reputation, lest by any means I might run, or had run, in vain. Yet not even Titus who *was* with me, being a Greek, was compelled to be circumcised. And *this occurred* because of false brethren secretly brought in (who came in by stealth to spy out our liberty which we have in Christ Jesus, that they might bring us into bondage), to whom we did not yield submission even for an hour, that the truth of the gospel might continue with you.

But from those who seemed to be something—whatever they were, it makes no difference to me; God shows personal favoritism to no man—for those who seemed *to be something* added nothing to me. But on the contrary, when they saw that the gospel for the uncircumcised had been committed to me, as *the gospel* for the circumcised *was* to Peter (for He who worked effectively in Peter for the apostleship to the circumcised also worked effectively in me toward the Gentiles), and when James, Cephas, and John, who seemed to be pillars, perceived the grace that had been given to me, they gave me and Barnabas the right hand of fellowship, that we *should go* to the Gentiles and they to the circumcised.." Galatians 2:1-9

Just as with proper doctrinal foundations, foundational church government will also allow Christ's building process to flourish. At this point we all must agree that Jesus is the Chief Cornerstone and Grand Architect of this thing we call the church. We who put our faith in Jesus Christ are the building. Yet, we are also called to be co-laborers in the building process. According to the grace of God that was given to him, Paul the apostle considered himself to be a wise master-builder who had laid the foundation. He admonished all who built upon it to do so with care (1 Corinthians 3:10). The apostle Peter also recites the theme.

"Coming to Him *as to* a living stone, rejected indeed by men, but chosen by God *and* precious, you also, as living stones, are being built up a spiritual house, a holy priesthood, to offer up spiritual sacrifices acceptable to God through Jesus Christ. Therefore it is also contained in the Scripture, *"Behold, I lay in Zion A chief cornerstone, elect, precious, And he who believes on Him will by no means be put to shame."* (1 Peter 2:4-6).

Why then have we so easily moved from this scriptural design to some other blueprint? Again, we have a tremendous capacity to build apart from God. Our traditional way of doing things often inadvertently causes us to limp along. Consider our structure in the Assemblies of God. Like other Pentecostal groups, when the A/G began to emerge, it was characterized as a fellowship of ministers (many, if not most, being alienated from existing denominations). Local church sovereignty was a high priority. The church demonstrated similar characteristics to the scattered church of Acts 8:1,4. Early on it was motivated to organize for the primary reasons of training ministers and facilitating missions. These are and continue to be noble and biblical causes. However, hierarchy and institutional structure began to develop. Avoiding denominational status, eventually the label was accepted. Though not intentional, hierarchy develops as ranks of ministry are recognized. More of this will be addressed shortly, but for now examples include full time verses part time ministers, graded credentials, senior pastors verses associate or assistant ministers, elected presbyteries and general/district council officers, boards and committees, and ultimately artificial distinction between clergy and laity. Clear admonition of scripture becomes clouded, "Yet it shall not be so among you; but whoever desires to become great among you, let him be your servant." (Matthew 20:26), "For I say, through the grace given to me, to everyone who is among you, not to think *of himself* more highly than he ought to think, but to think soberly, as God has dealt to each one a measure of faith." (Romans 12:3), "So then neither he who plants is anything, nor he who waters, but God who gives the increase." (1 Corinthians 3:7).

Concerning ministry roles/functions, because the pastoral/teaching gifts are more suited to prolonged local applications and are more abundant in number, they have traditionally been the most pervasive influence in local church settings (as expressed through local eldership). As a result, the other ministry gifts have tended to be de-emphasized.

Apostles, prophets, and evangelists are itinerate or transitional by design. Compared to local elders, they can be "on the go" or "on the way". Being misunderstood, they can be perceived as loose canons, flighty, non-relational, etc. In time they are usually considered irrelevant. Though they continue to function, the church tends to look upon them as "different". They make up a majority of those ministers who move (or are moved) from church to church, never really settling into their God-given roles. Sometimes they fit into that category of ministers who cannot seem to lead churches beyond a specific "plateau". They do not and should not fit the mold of pastor/teacher. They were designed to function differently. Before we return to "Heavenly Places and Beyond", some additional personal testimony may shed some light.

Chapter 7

"Heavenly Places and Beyond"
Ephesians 4:17-32
Death and Humility, Part 1

Not too long after we began to plant a church in 1980, a process began unfolding in my life as I started to understand the functional distinction in the ministry gifts. Previously, I was taught and I had observed the "perfecting" (other translations use the term "equipping") role of pastors, evangelists, and teachers as indicated in the above Scripture. Unfortunately, however, I was also instructed that the function of apostles and prophets (as described in these Scriptures) was not in operation today. There may be many reasons for this teaching of cessation. Here are three.

1) <u>Dispensationalism</u>. Though this is a valuable tool in hermeneutics, it has also been misused to deny a present day activity of apostles and prophets. Interestingly, Pentecostals and Charismatics decry this logic when used to explain away tongues and other manifestations of the Spirit, but then use it themselves to support their position concerning the ministry gifts. When the tradition of man replaces the revelation of scripture the church suffers. But the Reformation taught us that Christ will rule in His church. Thank God for the reformers who were bold enough to reopen truths that had been shelved for centuries. The scriptures do not speak of ministry roles terminating during this church age.

2) <u>Models based on tradition rather than scripture.</u> Again, man-made clerical distinctions and tradition cloud the issues. Catholics have generally labeled ministers as priests, cardinals, monks, abbots, etc…all with an attendant hierarchy. Protestants, though looking more carefully to scripture, have also developed ministry titles and models that lean toward a hierarchy (parson, reverend, rite reverend, presbyter, superintendent, general superintendent). However, scriptural definitions and examples lean toward a functional depiction of ministry roles.

3) <u>Abuse or exaggeration</u>. False apostles or prophets have led to their rejection out of hand. Apostles and prophets were never designated in Scripture in a hierarchal manner… order and function but not hierarchy. As will be pointed out in further discussion, if we will recognize all of the ministry gifts and submit to a scriptural pattern, Christ's foundation will be established.

Referring again to our church planting efforts in Duluth and beyond, we are in need of yielding our will to Jesus. In the Preface (p.9) I referred to team ministry and a plurality of elders that developed in our midst. For us, team ministry came about out of the revelation from Ephesians 4:11 that more than a pastor or group of pastors is given to the church by Jesus. If we were to embrace the other "five-fold" giftings we would have to identify more than one minister among us (or serving us from beyond our local) and discern what ministry gifts were distributed in our group. It is an on-going challenge to defer to Jesus as the Head of the church and to submit one to another as diverse functions are expressed. However, this "tension" is modeled to us in the New Testament as both a reality that Jesus left us with and a process that brings the church to maturity.

We adopted the New Testament pattern of a plurality of elders as well (Acts 14:23; Titus 1:5) and changed our bylaws from a congregational to elder form of government. This pattern of ordaining from within and calling from without gave additional opportunity for Jesus to reveal His five-fold ministry in our midst. Though our district superintendent did not try and discourage our changes (he in fact conceded that elder government appeared to be more scriptural) he shared his observation that the heart of man could frustrate even the best government structure. And indeed, in our midst, whenever one of our views or convictions becomes more prominent than discerning Christ's headship, we struggle.

A case in point involves identifying a head elder or pastor within a team of ministers. Though this has scriptural precedent (James in Jerusalem, Paul as a chief speaker, each of the respective "angels" in the seven churches addressed in Revelation) and can provide for order and direction even as a husband should in the marriage relationship, recognizing this person can be a struggle in grace. Also, it is important to remember that any distinction must be functional, not hierarchal. However, if humility is active in the process, grace will find a way and a humble servant will be identified. Again, Jesus admonished that the greatest would be he who served.

I am sure that in our desire to return to biblical patterns we have experienced our own pains of excess. At one point we had seven ordained or licensed ministers serving a congregation numbering less than one hundred. Over time the team began to disband, but this attempt resulted in several settings where team ministry/plurality exists to this day.

Other past experiences and observations illustrate the need to continually work toward scriptural patterns of ministry. Lack of success, especially when scripture and Holy Ghost conviction are driving us to seek solutions, can be most humbling. The following illustrations are intended to spur discussion for the benefit of rediscovering the need and utilization of a functionally diverse ministry based on Ephesians 4:11 designations rather than our own job descriptions.

Chapter 8

"Heavenly Places and Beyond"
Ephesians 4:17-32
Starving Our Apostles and Prophets

Recently I remarked to a fellow minister that when I answered the call to "church planting" in 1979 our District Home Missions Department recommended that I receive $300 per week as a salary. Thirty years later I am currently receiving no structured compensation from the churches I serve. I do not share this information to invoke sympathy but rather to illustrate the church's misdirected priorities. Should an apostle receive financial support from a church only when he serves as the pastor? Should larger churches that have multiple staff remunerate them at a higher rate of compensation than a smaller church simply because they have a larger financial base and can afford it? Should evangelists, prophets, or teachers who are itinerate in ministry have to make it on free will offerings? Should district or general council staff receive a more substantial or regulated "salary" than ministers who serve in local churches (regardless of their size)? Where do we get the notion that pay scales based on church size or educational attainment have validity in the church? Our corporate culture has influenced us heavily here. It has been commonly taught that churches are encouraged to set minister's salaries commensurate with scales of public school teachers, the median wage of church congregants, etc. We have all heard stories representing philosophies throughout the church community that espouse something like, "Lord, you keep the minister humble. We'll keep him poor."

On the other hand, scripture indicates that "elders that rule well be counted worthy of double honor (financial remuneration), especially they who labor in the word and doctrine" (1 Timothy 5:17). And in the following verse, "Thou shalt not muzzle the ox that treads out the corn. And the laborer is worthy of his reward". The example of believers bringing offerings and laying them at the apostles' feet would seem outlandish today, as would the idea of Paul receiving gifts from the Philippians when he was in Thessalonica (Philippians 4:15), or wealthier churches sending relief to needy churches (Acts 11:28-30; Galatians 2:9-10). In fairness, it should be noted that the Assemblies of God has applied many of these principles in various benevolent ministries and often excelled in these capacities through foreign and home missions. But it behooves us to revisit these topics on an on-going basis. There are indications that itinerate ministries served the early church in the administration of these types of things. The denominational trend of establishing more and more sophisticated levels of administration, departments, and attendant bureaucracies may end up sapping more resources than they distribute. But this is probably better left for another discussion.

Another indication of the need to identify five-fold giftings can be seen in the status accorded to ministers involved with pioneering efforts. Typically, younger… inexperienced ministers are called to plant churches. Success is measured by the rate of numerical growth. If this doesn't occur within a "reasonable" amount of time, the minister either moves on to a more lucrative position (to avoid long-term financial problems) or the supervising entity (Official Board, District/Section, mother church) begins to question the call or skills of this minister (not to mention the minister's own struggles with failure). Or the previously described "misunderstood" or "non-descript" minister labors in relative obscurity, accomplishing only a fraction of what could potentially be achieved if teamed up with other gifted ministers.

What are the root issues of this scenario? First, because of our tradition that size equals success, we create an environment that states "church planting or pioneering is for rookies". It is one of those starting rungs on the ladder of ministry. Second, pastors who do not fit "the mold" somehow find themselves involved with church plants. Even our boot camp equipping philosophy is geared to this. Though the concepts developed in these camps may have much value, the working philosophy is flawed. It has been borrowed from our culture. Basically it states, "we can develop church planters and hence plant churches if we train these younger ministers (or retrain the unsuccessful types) to apply proven church growth principles in any given community". Again, growth is the yardstick for success.

However, an historical note adds perspective here. The story is told about Waldo Trask and his church planting ministry in Grand Rapids, MN a number of decades ago. After a sustained effort to start an Assembly of God church in that community, he and his wife moved on without apparent success. In fact, when leaving the city, Mrs. Trask asked Waldo to pull their vehicle to the side of the road. Mrs. Trask proceeded to exit the vehicle and symbolically shake the dust from her feet, stating that Grand Rapids had rejected their gospel witness. Perhaps that was the case. However, I would suggest an additional perspective. Because the greater church lacked insight into the primary importance of the Trask's ministry, the resources were not provided to sustain the term required to see the church develop autonomy in the community. The Trask's indeed planted, with great personal sacrifice, as many ministers do. What they accomplished in the "heavenly places" will ultimately be reviewed in eternity. But what they began, primarily in the unseen realm, provided a foundation for a church that later appeared…and today is very strong. This can be said of other communities in Minnesota and beyond where "successful" churches now exist, yet saw limited results from the Trask's efforts. What would have happened if the Trask's were adequately funded and recognized concerning the priority of their work? What would have happened if other apostolic or prophetic ministers could have been resourced to strengthen the Trasks' mission? What would happen if the church truly understood the foundational role of apostles and prophets, supporting them accordingly, and encouraging an environment in which they could not only labor to the completion of their function but equip others to do the same? Instead, ministers like them are destined to literally start from scratch every time they embark on a new mission to bring the church into existence in an un-reached community or bring order in the midst of a struggling core of believers.

When we first attended bible college in 1975, my family and I had the privilege to serve under Wilbert Johnson. Wilbert had assumed the pastorate of North St. Paul Assembly of God. Sometime after coming into this position, he discovered a letter from the District that had been left in the church office before his tenure began announcing that the church had officially been closed. Fortunately he was not privy to this and he faithfully answered God's call to rebuild. My young family and I came to this fellowship in search of a church that we could attend during our bible college training.

Little did we know that apostleship would be modeled to us. At great personal cost, with little or no recognition, Brother Johnson and his family labored to build this church. Before and during our brief stay, prophesies were given that God would send people from the North, South, East, and West. In fact, the night that we first attended (the pastor and a handful of congregants were present) we were welcomed with royal treatment, as if long lost family had come home. After our departure to pursue further training, Brother Johnson and his fledgling church began to reach out to the newly arriving Hmong community that were emigrating from Southeast Asia to St. Paul. It would later be noted by some in that community that Brother Johnson was the apostle of Pentecost to the Hmong. The work of grace that characterized Wilbert's life was filled with faith, servant-hood, and sacrifice... among other notable qualities. But his apostolic gifting did not elevate him to a prominent pastorate of a large church. Instead, his ministry gave birth to the church of Pentecost among the Hmong people and made room for other ministers to step into more traditional pastoral roles.

This gives rise to a statement I find myself using more often as I observe apostolic ministry (prophets and evangelists can be included in this as well), "apostles are at best transitional". Their effectiveness not only comes into play when churches are staring but also at key junctures in church life.

Acts 8:14-ff records that the apostles Peter and John were sent to Samaria to confirm and add to the work begun by the evangelist Philip. They then returned to Jerusalem. This pattern continued after Paul was converted, Barnabas taking Paul under his wing Acts 9:26-31, and later the two being sent out from Antioch (Acts 13). It seemed natural (or should I say, supernatural) for them and the church to allow their gifts to flourish in this way.

A picture of what would be unheard of today can be found in Acts 14. Paul and Barnabas were instrumentally used by God to bring the gospel to Lycaonia, see at least several local churches born (v.23), and then turn the work over to elders whom they had ordained...all in a matter of months! Do we see this type of gifting in operation today? No we do not, at least not in our western culture. Instead, we recruit a "home missions pastor" or "church planter" often without considering his particular ministry gift. Bible college graduation is often the entry level preparation for those pursuing this activity. After putting him through a boot camp where we've introduced him to successful models/methods, we ask him to do what God intended a team of gifted ministers to accomplish. The trend promoted in our boot camps to develop a church planting team is a step in the right direction. However, replacing scriptural designations of ministry gifts with terms like missionary (home or foreign) limits the scope of God's design. In addition our contrived methods tend to erase the spontaneity that characterized New Testament church expansion. "Wild Fire" church growth has been replaced by tradition and methodology that is motivated by the need to control. Again, Paul's statement to the Ephesian elders has practically become way beyond our systematic ability to comprehend.

> "So now, brethren, I commend you to God and to the word of His grace, which is able to build you up and give you an inheritance among all those who are sanctified." Acts 20:32

We have an opportunity and a responsibility to submit our building efforts to the pattern in God's word . Can we? Will we? I believe it is possible if we continue on the path of death and humility.

Chapter 9
"Heavenly Places and Beyond"
Ephesians 4:17-32
Death and Humility, Part 2

At the risk of being misunderstood, I again offer my own testimony as a further example. I do so because I believe it is representative of a host of ministers in our movement who have had similar experiences, many of which have never been observed from this perspective.

In the early years of what I used to call church planting, I did not understand why I was consumed with the desire to birth new churches and minister in multiple settings. At one juncture I was sharing my compulsion with our presbyter, stating how I did not know if I could stand by another year without starting another church. He tried to console me by saying he had waited over ten years without seeing his vision come to pass (goals and dreams of seeing the church he served relocate and build a new facility).

During that time I was "planting vicariously" by encouraging several other ministers to start churches in our community. In some ways it was like shooting myself in the foot. Because when another church started, it only prolonged the time when I could again do it again first hand. I even started ministry at two local colleges praying about seeing churches on campus instead of campus ministries representing denominations. I can remember viewing my times there as an "escape" from the constraints of pastoral ministry.

Along the way I was denied the opportunity on two occasions to start new churches. The church I was currently serving as "pastor" was as frustrated as I was. My vision was to fields beyond, working locally to pass my baton to others, in order that I might move on.

During this mix of things, I approached our Sectional and District officers with a team approach. The elders I served with and I would assume ministry responsibility over one of the failing new churches. During our deliberations one of the newer ministers to our area stepped forward, stating that God was calling him to now lead that home missions effort! Of course, the system and our tradition lent it to going that way.

About a year later, after this pastor (he was actually professing to be an evangelist, and probably was) moved on, we applied again with the same plan. I now received the "home missions appointment". With it came the "home missions status", the fledgling ministry identity, etc. But eventually we developed a separate team of elders and deacons at the second church, incorporated and became a sovereign assembly within our District. However, both churches continued to maintain close relationship, especially on the eldership level. In fact the first church continued to provide a good portion of my personal financial support (though it never received World Ministries credit for it).

During this entire process we searched near and far, within and without the Assemblies of God, trying to find like-minded churches and leaders who shared our vision. On at least two occasions we spoke to our Section ministers and District officials to quell rumors that were developing about our unorthodox methods and government. One pastor of a larger church in our Section even "counseled" at least one younger minister to stay clear and not associate with us. Outside of the A/G, wherever we found "like-minded brothers", without exception we were invited to join up with these other groups. Their view was that the path we were on would not be allowed by the A/G. And indeed I have received numbers of exhortations from A/G ministers to cease and desist from pursuing this model. However, this all has served as a kind of prophetic urging to continue in the face of opposition, trusting that the Lord would reconcile these differences for His purposes (Ephesians 4:13-16).

Several years later, with a growing ministry team, we assumed ministry responsibility over a third failing home missions work, again with the same "starting over" scenario. With the team approach of plural eldership now functioning in the second church, both churches were supportive of this new effort. There were now six local elders in our leadership structure that served the first two churches. And we were developing relationships with a number of apostles, evangelists, prophets., pastors and teachers from without our local settings..

A side bar to this developing ministry philosophy was our growing conviction that the cell church model was best suited to our evangelism and discipleship efforts. This in itself could provide an in depth discussion which cannot be pursued in this writing. Then came what I now believe was a mistake that has in many respects hampered our efforts to this day.

The head elder (pastor) of the second church "prophetically" suggested that because we were attempting to multiply according to a cell church model, it might be best for us to merge the three churches, believing that by centralizing administratively, we could continue to multiply through cell groups rather than starting local churches over and over again. After prayer and deliberation the growing eldership that served each respective church came together, indeed believing that this was God's will.

I believe our mistake came by not sticking with the functional gifting distributed among us as elders. I was invited by the others to serve as the "pastor" or "head elder" of this merged church, not being true to what I now understand to be the apostolic call on my life. Whether it was pride or the pressure to grow by any means I do not know. But God, who is faithful according to His prescription to accomplish His purpose (Romans 8:28-ff), is not limited by our "mistakes". Establishing the local church in any and every distinct community should be our goal. Ordaining elders (developing a plurality that allows five-fold gifting to function) brings Christ's government to bear through loving service (1 Peter 5:1-4) and protects both the eldership and church from impending peril (Acts 20:28-31).

At this point the ministry team (now numbering seven) that I alluded to earlier entered into a renewed effort to walk out a functionally diverse team ministry. This is how it looked. Two of us ultimately shared apostolic gifting (one transitioning from more of a prophetic role), another prophet, three pastors and teachers, and an evangelist. These seven diversely gifted men came alive for a season with energy and vision that inspires me to this day. Another group of seven formed a deaconate that served along side of us. Then the process of death and humility began to unfold its work in our midst. In our zeal for diversity I believe we began to miss the Headship of Christ in our midst. As argued earlier, only Jesus can build the true church through members who submit to Him as the Head and to one another as fellow laborers. Church government breaks down in any setting where this is not observed.

In our case it was at first subtle and eventually blatant. Rather than place blame upon myself or others, a tendency that I share with most of humanity, here I choose to describe our struggle from a different perspective...one that identifies our common dilemma. It is always easier to vicariously view someone else's journey of death and humility when indeed Christ invites us to participate in His. As we do, His life mysteriously appears in us and through us.

In our situation, several different views and visions began to emerge from among the elders concerning our cell church development. Also, personal tensions among the elders were not relationally settled. Both of these should cause us to reflect again upon Paul's admonition to elders to take heed to themselves and to the flock over which God has made them overseers. Even though we visited these themes often in our discussions, we were then unable to "view the forest for the trees".

Again, without assigning blame, it will be helpful here to discuss our journey to this day. The brother who first suggested that we merge ended up moving to another state to join a non-A/G church planting effort . I ultimately resigned out of conviction that I was "pushing" some of my fellow elders in a direction they were uncomfortable with, particularly concerning the subject of aggressive cell group expansion. But also the urge to minister in fields beyond could again not be denied. My resignation was accepted by the other elders with the provision that I serve until a new head elder/pastor was installed. One of the elders who demonstrates clear pastoral gifting serves in that capacity to the day of this writing.

While several other elders have been raised up in that setting over the last ten years, six others have moved on to other church settings. One of them is my son-in-law who is now serving as head elder/pastor in another church we have since started in our present community. Currently there are five credentialed ministers and several others aspiring/preparing for elder and five-fold ministry on our two campuses. Our primary goal is to facilitate the development of "next generation" ministers in our midst while simultaneously seeing every member discipled for the work God assigns to them.

Back to that part of the story, my personal role in this process looks like this. Upon completion of seeing the church in Duluth resting in the care of the remaining elders and new pastor, my family and I moved, leaving the city which we had believed would be our base for life. The church there continues to recognize me as an "extra-local" elder functioning as an apostle, leaving the door open for relational ministry. Today, ten years later, my role with that church continues to develop and strengthen.

With our relocation we began to pursue what is developing into more of an itinerant ministry, building and strengthening the church wherever God called us. The result has been serving three congregations in our Section (each for a year each) in an interim capacity, assisting in a church plant in Chicago, building ministry ties in several other churches, and starting a church in the community where we now reside. God also opened doors to make ministry trips to India and Europe, where we believe God is preparing us to return. These activities generally have over lapped or taken place simultaneously. While also "assisting" the current pastor in our second campus, we are looking for ways to continue work near and far as God calls and opens doors. Additional testimony will follow about how God is calling us to Europe, India, Mexico and beyond.

In each of the interim positions previously mentioned, my main objective was to "set things in order" while continuing to "pastor" the new church we were starting in our home community. In all these places of ministry my goal has been to identify and equip other ministers who can continue building the church. Some things are changing in the process but with great struggle from my perspective. First, I have come to a place in my life where I must be brutally honest with myself and others concerning my calling. Because I am an apostle, my role is different that that of a pastor. Some within the churches I serve and in the Assemblies of God reject this out of hand. However I must function as God has called and graced me, leaving the results with God. I increasingly understand that my role best serves the church transitionally or temporarily, though this provides great challenges logistically and financially. Continued misunderstanding and even criticism from peers and those within our hierarchal structure give fresh reality to the "stigma" I referenced earlier. But the fruit continues to out-weigh the investment. The church is being strengthened, men and women are answering God's call into ministry, the gospel of the Kingdom is touching previously unreached people and areas, souls are being added to the church and becoming disciples.

In 2008 I had the privilege of traveling to Europe with my wife and our two youngest children after more than two decades of prayerful consideration. The burden to do this developed as a result of my father and my wife's great grandfather emigrating from Europe in the early 1900's, our family members traveling there in the past, and believing that our European relatives have not had a clear presentation of the gospel. As God graciously gave us the opportunity to bring the gospel to our known and unknown relatives there, the highlight of the trip was seeing more than thirty family members in Italy, Slovenia, and Croatia profess their faith in the Lord Jesus Christ. Sadly, there are very few New Testament churches in the thousands of rural villages and towns throughout Europe.

In preparation for the trip I had contacted missionaries who served in fields where we would be visiting, offering any help we could bring to the churches. It seems that they were "not structured" to accommodate how/where we could be of service while traveling through their areas. Warnings were even issued concerning distrust that some of the national churches had toward visitors. One country even discouraged us from making any contact with the churches.

As we journeyed through a rural setting in Italy searching for my wife's family roots, we stopped repeatedly for directions and ended up quite off the beaten path. At a very obscure café, while simultaneously receiving directions from four Italians who could not speak English (we also do not understand Italian), two men walked in who began to assist us. One of them spoke a little English and proceeded to tell us that he was actually French but now was serving in Italy as an itinerate minister. I likewise briefly shared our testimony and purpose for being there. Immediately we exchanged the customary kisses and hugs, and in this case the reality of Christian fellowship, to which the locals wondered at considering our newfound connection with these strangers. We continued to discuss our respective missions and callings.

It turns out that this man and his family are functioning in a similar fashion to our ministry...and facing almost identical issues. Living near Florence, he was on his way (when we met him) to minister in Naples at a church that had required one hundred attempts to start. Consisting largely of former mafia members, this church is part of a growing network that is endeavoring to build upon New Testament principles. After receiving directions, we were invited to return to Naples on the morrow and minister in testimony and song. Later the congregation prayed for our return trip to my wife's family's village where we were blessed to have several relatives and strangers profess faith in Christ in response to our testimonies. Also, after the service and before we traveled to that location, we were referred to better accommodations, invited into the home of one of the congregants, and later saw one of their family members profess faith in Christ in response to our gospel appeal.

After our ultimate destination to Slovenia and in route back home, we were invited to spend the night in the home of our newly found partner in ministry. Jointly we believe that God has called us to labor together in Italy and beyond at some future point, trusting that God ordained our meeting and desires us to walk in works He has prepared for us.

We had similar experiences in Slovenia and Croatia where family members have long since separated from the church as they know it, yet displayed great spiritual hunger and interest in our testimony of Christ's gospel. Professions of Christ occurred here as well; yet again we found little or no local church structure that we could plug them into. We are prayerfully waiting on God to open return trips to these places to establish and strengthen the church.

This parallels the experience I referenced earlier to the two apostles I met in India. I believe that God has designed these encounters to encourage me in my calling and to encourage the church world wide to respond to his grace.

It is my prayerful purpose to continue reaching beyond any local church I serve in these United States as well as return to ministry situations in Europe, India, Mexico and anywhere else God calls me to establish and strengthen His church. I am sure that I will learn more than I impart as I go. Yet, going will release additional grace to encourage other foundational ministers.

God's desire and purpose is to extend His Kingdom through the ministry of the gospel. As apostles and other fivefold ministers continue to walk in His grace…as the body is continually equipped to walk in each member's respective calling...we will experience the reality of dwelling in heavenly places and beyond. The existence and calling of the church does not end with our time upon the earth. We are on our way unto the measure of the stature of the fullness of Christ.

More specifically, we must hear what the Spirit is saying to the church corporately and individually. Jesus is declared to be the one who walks in the midst of the candlesticks (the churches) in Revelation 2:1. As He repeated some key exhortations to the church, we too can benefit by revisiting some thoughts discussed earlier.

Chapter 10

Heavenly Places and Beyond
Consider Your calling

It can be argued that when father Abraham spoke of "… the city which has foundations, whose builder and maker is God" (Hebrews 11:10), he was in a type describing the church. Romans 4:1-18 indicates that his spiritual descendents would include Jew and Gentile alike. Additionally, Ephesians 2 groups the believing Jews and Gentiles into that entity we call the church, verses 19 – 21 ending this way,

> Now, therefore, you are no longer strangers and foreigners, but fellow citizens with the saints and members of the household of God, having been built on the foundation of the apostles and prophets, Jesus Christ Himself being the chief corner*stone,* in whom the whole building, being fitted together, grows into a holy temple in the Lord,

Whether you are part of a denomination, a restoration movement, an independent assembly, or a house church... if you are calling on Jesus as your Lord and Savior...Jesus alone must be the foundation. And because He sets us in the church as it pleases Him (1 Corinthians 12:18), Jesus will continue changing us until we come into conformance with His plan (Ephesians 4:13). As stated at the onset, we are now a building under construction, inhabited by God through the Spirit. We shall be the bride, the Lamb's wife, that holy city in which the Lord God Almighty and the Lamb are the temple, as described in Revelation21: 9-27.

> Then one of the seven angels who had the seven bowls filled with the seven last plagues came to me and talked with me, saying, "Come, I will show you the bride, the Lamb's wife." And he carried me away in the Spirit to a great and high mountain, and showed me the great city, the holy Jerusalem, descending out

of heaven from God, having the glory of God. Her light *was* like a most precious stone, like a jasper stone, clear as crystal. Also she had a great and high wall with twelve gates, and twelve angels at the gates, and names written on them, which are *the names* of the twelve tribes of the children of Israel: three gates on the east, three gates on the north, three gates on the south, and three gates on the west. Now the wall of the city had twelve foundations, and on them were the names of the twelve apostles of the Lamb. And he who talked with me had a gold reed to measure the city, its gates, and its wall. The city is laid out as a square; its length is as great as its breadth. And he measured the city with the reed: twelve thousand furlongs. Its length, breadth, and height are equal. Then he measured its wall: one hundred *and* forty-four cubits, *according* to the measure of a man, that is, of an angel. The construction of its wall was *of* jasper; and the city *was* pure gold, like clear glass. The foundations of the wall of the city *were* adorned with all kinds of precious stones: the first foundation *was* jasper, the second sapphire, the third chalcedony, the fourth emerald, the fifth sardonyx, the sixth sardius, the seventh chrysolite, the eighth beryl, the ninth topaz, the tenth chrysoprase, the eleventh jacinth, and the twelfth amethyst. The twelve gates *were* twelve pearls: each individual gate was of one pearl. And the street of the city *was* pure gold, like transparent glass.

But I saw no temple in it, for the Lord God Almighty and the Lamb are its temple. The city had no need of the sun or of the moon to shine in it, for the glory of God illuminated it. The Lamb *is* its light. And the nations of those who are saved shall walk in its light, and the kings of the earth bring their glory and honor into it. Its gates shall not be shut at all by day (there shall be no night there). And they shall bring the glory and the honor of the nations into it. But there shall by no means enter it anything that defiles, or causes an abomination or a lie, but only those who are written in the Lamb's Book of Life.

It is understood that this perspective includes a rather grand sweep of ecclesiology. Amazingly though, much (most?) of the church today is not practically conscious of the fact that we are experiencing a major renovation carried out by none other than Jesus Himself. Why? Again, it is because so many lives are built around Christ, not on Christ. As we revisit the theme that man has always had a tremendous capacity to build apart from God, consider again the earlier reference to Babel, when they said,

"Come, let us build ourselves a city, and a tower whose top *is* in the heavens; let us make a name for ourselves, lest we be scattered abroad over the face of the whole earth." (Genesis 11:4).

We can apply the same principle that Paul shared with the Corinthians,

"Now all these things happened to them as examples, and they were written for our admonition, upon whom the ends of the ages have come." 1 Corinthians 10:11

Psalms 11:3 and 82:5 warn of ignoring the foundation.

"If the foundations are destroyed, What can the righteous do? They do not know, nor do they understand; They walk about in darkness; All the foundations of the earth are unstable.

Man continues to build with much ingenuity under a religious guise. In fact, the ultimate religious effort will be a self-perpetuating heap of false building.

"For the time will come when they will not endure sound doctrine, but according to their own desires, *because* they have itching ears, they will heap up for themselves teachers." 2 Timothy 4:3

When explaining the building process, Paul stated that "Everyman's work shall be made manifest..." (I Corinthians 3:13). He also exhorted that,

"As you therefore have received Christ Jesus the Lord, so walk in Him, rooted and built up in Him... Let no one cheat you of your reward... and not holding fast to the Head, from whom all the body...grows with the increase *that is* from God." (Colossians 2:6-7,18-19, excerpts).

Individual, personal faith in Christ has no substitute. Continued conformity to His image ultimately fulfills His will (Romans 8:28-29).

Ponder these propositions again.

1) In addition to The Foundation, Scripture speaks also about the building process being foundational.

> "I planted, Apollos watered, but God gave the increase. According to the grace of God which was given to me, as a wise master builder I have laid the foundation, and another builds on it. But let each one take heed how he builds on it." (I Corinthians 3:6,10).

2) When compared to the earlier quoted phrase from Ephesians 2:20, "...the foundation of the apostles and prophets...", it is evident that Paul and other apostles and prophets were given grace to do foundational ministry. Understanding this functional distinction in the ministry gifts greatly enhances the role of ministers as described in Ephesians 4:7-16.

> "But to each one of us grace was given according to the measure of Christ's gift. Therefore He says: *"When He ascended on high, He led captivity captive, And gave gifts to men."* (Now this, *"He ascended"* — what does it mean but that He also first descended into the lower parts of the earth? He who descended is also the One who ascended far above all the heavens, that He might fill all

things.) And He Himself gave some *to be* apostles, some prophets, some evangelists, and some pastors and teachers, for the equipping of the saints for the work of ministry, for the edifying of the body of Christ, till we all come to the unity of the faith and of the knowledge of the Son of God, to a perfect man, to the measure of the stature of the fullness of Christ; that we should no longer be children, tossed to and fro and carried about with every wind of doctrine, by the trickery of men, in the cunning craftiness of deceitful plotting, but, speaking the truth in love, may grow up in all things into Him who is the head— Christ— from whom the whole body, joined and knit together by what every joint supplies, according to the effective working by which every part does its share, causes growth of the body for the edifying of itself in love."

Pride has a way of blinding us to the truth. We will be better served to heed the examples of Old Testament failure where men refused to admit that their ways and practices had swerved from God's revealed truth. Christ is the chief cornerstone. Jesus has given apostles and prophets to His church. Again, thank God that an ever-increasing portion of the body of Christ is recognizing and responding to this truth. And again, this generation is witnessing both the laying of new foundations through a proliferation of church planting and a renovation of existing church structure. As warned in 1 Corinthians 3:12-15, let us build in faith and truth.

> "Now if anyone builds on this foundation *with* gold, silver, precious stones, wood, hay, straw, each one's work will become clear; for the Day will declare it, because it will be revealed by fire; and the fire will test each one's work, of what sort it is. If anyone's work which he has built on *it* endures, he will receive a reward. If anyone's work is burned, he will suffer loss; but he himself will be saved, yet so as through fire."

Every man's work will be made manifest. What is your role? Are you building upon the foundation using a foundational process? Or are you working on the last days' Tower of Babel? As we walk in our calling, two other perspectives can be considered here…circumventing the call of God and the mini church movement.

Chapter 11

Heavenly Places and Beyond Circumventing the Call of God

"As they ministered to the Lord and fasted, the Holy Spirit said, "Now separate to Mc Barnabas and Saul for the work to which I have called them." Then, having fasted and prayed, and laid hands on them, they sent *them* away." Acts 13:2,3

It doesn't get more spontaneous yet purposeful than this… spontaneous in the immediacy of the disciples' response to the Holy Spirit and the manner in which He spoke, yet purposeful both in their ministry to the Lord and His plan to extend the church.

The call of God is a mysterious and wonderful activity. It is rooted in ages past. "Moreover whom He predestined, these He also called..." Romans 8:30(a) "...just as He chose us in Him before the foundation of the world..." Ephesians 1:4(a) But the call of implementation is the truth set forth in Ephesians 2:10. "For we are His workmanship, created in Christ Jesus for good works, which God prepared beforehand that we should walk in them."

We must believe and anticipate that He will guide us into preordained works. This is the same spirit that Jesus manifested when He said, "My Father has been working until now, and I have been working." John 5:17. Stephen did the same in Acts 6:8, "And Stephen, full of faith and power, did great wonders and signs among the people.", as did Philip in (Acts 8:6) "And the multitudes with one accord heeded the things spoken by Philip, hearing and seeing the miracles which he did.", and Peter toward Cornelius's household (Acts 10:19-20)

"While Peter thought about the vision, the Spirit said to him, "Behold, three men are seeking you. Arise therefore, go down and go with them, doubting nothing; for I have sent them."

Paul and his team certainly demonstrated this when redirected by the Holy Spirit to go into Europe instead of Asia (Acts 16:6-10).

> "Now when they had gone through Phrygia and the region of Galatia, they were forbidden by the Holy Spirit to preach the word in Asia. After they had come to Mysia, they tried to go into Bithynia, but the Spirit did not permit them. So passing by Mysia, they came

down to Troas. And a vision appeared to Paul in the night. A man of Macedonia stood and pleaded with him, saying, 'Come over to Macedonia and help us.' Now after he had seen the vision, immediately we sought to go to Macedonia, concluding that the Lord had called us to preach the gospel to them."

But the bigger the ship, the more time and space that is required to turn. Methods and programs can easily become part of a Babel syndrome. Cultural success has a way of us focusing on what man esteems rather than what God deems vital. The seven churches of Revelation again serve as examples of what Christ desires. He reminded Ephesus of her first works and love. He called Smyrna to faithfulness amidst poverty and suffering. Pergamos was chastened for doctrinal impurity even though she was faithful to Christ's name. Thyatira's works, charity, service, and faith were threatened by Jezebel's infiltration. Sardis was dead even though her name proclaimed life. Philadelphia was exhorted to hold fast what remained. And Laodicea was to be spued out of Christ's mouth for being luke warm, blinded to her nakedness and poverty by her riches and self-sufficiency. As a church or denomination grows can it remain both spontaneous and purposeful?

In the Assemblies of God, two things may help us address the need as just described. Other church groups can benefit as well. The first has to do with our administrative development on the Sectional, District, and General Council levels. These areas of our structure are increasingly hierarchal in nature and development. Contrast that to the founders of the A/G who gathered as a fellowship of ministers. Our early leaders saw the need to organize more broadly, particularly to facilitate world missions and ministerial training. This must continue. However, the emphasis must return to empowering and resourcing the local church and the release of gifted ministry.

> "Then the churches throughout all Judea, Galilee, and Samaria had peace and were edified. And walking in the fear of the Lord and in the comfort of the Holy Spirit, they were multiplied." Acts 9:31

Just as in our physical bodies, multiplication and the related factors are built into the churches' DNA.

Our relatively recent recognition of the need and Scriptural privilege/responsibility of local churches to ordain elders/ministers is a tremendous step in this direction. By no means does this say that training and ordination at other levels in our structure is wrong. We must continue these emphases. But our Sections and District/General Councils need to return to our original parameters, namely: fellowship, training, and resourcing…not directing, initiating, and defining. Our resources are vast. God has increasingly put within our control the ability to fund, train, and facilitate. But we must rethink the size and requirements of our administration, limiting them and channeling our wealth throughout the grassroots of our movement…the local churches. Instead we are constantly prone to additionally leverage the local churches to serve central administrative structure.

The apostolic movement in Australia apparently has tried to address this by renewed scriptural emphasis upon the function of apostles. However, weakness in their "progress" may take a wrong turn if unscriptural hierarchal authority is assigned to apostolic gifting. The earlier section dealing with functional church government needs to be kept in mind here. Our tendency to vest greater authority in our elected presbyters and District/General Council officers flies in the face of New Testament patterns. So does an emphasis upon any particular ministry gift. Paul's testimony in Galatians 2 directly challenges a hierarchal structure of authority in the church. Without desiring to be redundant, but rather to add emphasis, let it be stated again. There is only one Head in the church and that is the Lord Jesus Christ. All other authority is delegated and functional. Anything beyond that infringes upon Peter's admonition to "…nor as being lords over those entrusted to you, but being examples to the flock" 1 Peter 5:3. Oversight works best from a functional perspective, rooted in loving service.

Let it again be stated at this juncture that these perspectives are in no way intended to impugn our presbyteries or any individuals in our present governmental system. It is the structure…the wineskin that is being examined. We are blessed to have God gifted men/women who serve throughout our fellowship, both in the local churches and our district/general councils. This appeal is to refine the structure, to re-examine our function with a fresh hard look at scriptural patterns…the Bible being after all our authority for faith and practice.

Chapter 12

Heavenly Places and Beyond The Mini-church Movement

One other area is strategically related as we try not to circumvent God's call and our ability to respond to it. That has to do with the size of our churches. Before I was saved (1953-1973), I grew up in a local parish comprised of about fifteen hundred (1,500) families situated in a town of about eight thousand (8,000) people. That church did not teach about being born again, nor did it emphasize many of the other doctrines that we consider fundamental. But size dictated power, and hierarchal administrative control was strong.

Since entering the Assemblies of God in 1974, I have witnessed the emergence of the mega church mentality in our movement. Big churches have benefited us in many ways. But is big necessarily better? Is church growth and success now predicated upon the size of the local church? I'm afraid we are on a slippery slope as this thought develops. Yet we train our ministers to aspire toward building super churches. Our guest speakers at conferences, camps, and bible colleges are generally from large "successful" ministries. Our structure rewards growth-based success and promotion based on numbers. We mostly qualify success by the size of a church. We qualify a minister's abilities by the size of the church he can grow. But scripture says,

> Who then is Paul, and who *is* Apollos, but ministers through whom you believed, as the Lord gave to each one? I planted, Apollos watered, but God gave the increase. So then neither he who plants is anything, nor he who waters, but God who gives the increase. Now he who plants and he who waters are one, and each one will receive his own reward according to his own labor. For we are God's fellow workers; you are God's field, *you are* God's building. 1 Corinthians 3:5-9

> "For I say, through the grace given to me, to everyone who is among you, not to think *of himself* more highly than he ought to think, but to think soberly, as God has dealt to each one a measure of faith." Romans 12:3

"For we dare not class ourselves or compare ourselves with those who commend themselves. But they, measuring themselves by themselves, and comparing themselves among themselves, are not wise." 2 Corinthians 10:12

"I sent you to reap that whereon you bestowed no labor; other men labored, and you are entered into their labors." I sent you to reap that for which you have not labored; others have labored, and you have entered into their labors." John 4:38

Big can be good. We should rejoice when multiplication occurs in this way. We should encourage those who are given the privilege and responsibility of a great harvest because they can be pressed beyond measure. But small can be good, too. The fact is that the majority of churches in our movement and others are small churches. Statistics show that most of the communities that do not yet have an Assembly of God church are smaller communities. Even in our metropolitan centers smaller churches make up the majority.

Hence I propose that the "Mini Church Movement" needs to be celebrated as much as the "Mega Church Movement". Let us again recognize that "… the gifts and the calling of God *are* irrevocable." Romans 11:29 Let us remember again Paul's admonition,

"For I say, through the grace given to me, to everyone who is among you, not to think *of himself* more highly than he ought to think, but to think soberly, as God has dealt to each one a measure of faith." Romans 12:3

With that in mind, consider this. The vast majority of kingdom activity in the church takes place in smaller gatherings and in smaller churches. Shouldn't we be directing a proportionate amount of our energies and resources among that majority? Should our larger churches and their efforts receive the greater focus of our resources and the greater accolades because their individual successes may be more visible? I think not. Yes, we should rejoice with the big. But we should also rejoice with the small. We do at times give lip service to this, but our focus, resourcing, and energies tell another story. Zechariah 4:10 speaks to us, "For who has despised the day of small things?" It would serve us well to walk out the theme verse posted on every Pentecostal Evangel, "...

'Not by might nor by power, but by My Spirit,' Says the LORD of hosts" Zechariah 4:6(b). Have we forgotten what 1 Corinthians 1:26-31 considers?

"For you see your calling, brethren, that not many wise according to the flesh, not many mighty, not many noble, *are called.* But God has chosen the foolish things of the world to put to shame the wise, and God has chosen the weak things of the world to put to shame the things which are mighty; and the base things of the world and the things which are despised God has chosen, and the things which are not, to bring to nothing the things that are, that no flesh should glory in His presence. But of Him you are in Christ Jesus, who became for us wisdom from God—and righteousness and sanctification and redemption—that, as it is written, *"He who glories, let him glory in the LORD.."*

Here are a few suggestions that can help us celebrate and build within the "Mini Church Movement".

1) Let us recognize that many our most gifted ministers serve in our smaller churches. They are there by a combination of God's design, ("But now God has set the members, each one of them, in the body just as He pleased.") 1 Corinthians 12:18, and apportioned stewardship ("And to one he gave five talents, to another two, and to another one...") Matthew 25:15. Theirs may be an appointed season of sowing and watering.

"So then neither he who plants is anything, nor he who waters, but God who gives the increase. Now he who plants and he who waters are one, and each one will receive his own reward according to his own labor." 1 Corinthians 3:7-8

God's dispensation of grace may involve a smaller portion of His flock.

For if I do this willingly, I have a reward; but if against my will, I have been entrusted with a stewardship (alternate KJV '...a dispensation of the gospel is committed unto me.')" 1 Corinthians 9:17)

2) Let us encourage larger churches and our Districts/General Council to underwrite missions projects and personnel in smaller churches with "no strings attached". Why should smaller churches and ministers with less influence have a higher standard of accountability than their larger counterparts? This will require that the ordination/credential status of those in smaller settings is as valid as those in larger settings. It will also recognize that God sets a diversely gifted ministry in those settings, and that they by design may be better suited to work in those settings than in larger ones. Consider that the price of adding another staff member in a larger church may underwrite an entire church plant in a smaller setting. Will larger churches, Districts and the General Council consider down sizing present administrative resources, utilizing more unpaid members, and releasing greater numbers of bi-vocational ministers in an effort to expand the kingdom beyond their own tent?

3) Let us invite ministers from our "mini churches" to minister at our bible colleges, conferences, camps, etc., not

just in workshop settings, but even as plenary speakers and lead participants.

4) Let us repent of our respect of persons and recognize that God <u>truly</u> values his ministers at all levels and every segment of His body.

It behooves us to walk on to the maturity written about in Ephesians. As earlier mentioned, there are the prepared works (2:10) and the walk that is worthy (4:1). In addition we are not to walk as other Gentiles, in the vanity of their mind (4:17). But we are to walk in love, as Christ (5:2). The slogan of recent years is very appropriate here. What would Jesus do? We must walk as children of light (5:8). Lastly we must walk circumspectly (5:15). From this term is derived the word acrobat. Yes, we are to walk as acrobats...with much skill and carefulness. As we continue to walk in our calling, a picture develops of how a Christian and hence the church looks.

Chapter 13

"Heavenly Places and Beyond" What Does A Christian Look Like?
Ephesians 5:1-20

Thus far we've been told by the apostle Paul that we the church are <u>chosen</u> before the foundation of the world to be holy ones, faithful, <u>presently blessed</u> with all spiritual blessings in heavenly places in Christ, <u>sealed</u> with the Holy Spirit of promise until the redemption of the purchased possession, that in the ages to come He might show the exceeding riches of His grace.

This all happens by grace through faith in Christ's finished work. Are you NOW living in heavenly places? Are you NOW walking in grace? Are you NOW enjoying the blessings of your inheritance as God's child? Are you NOW being indwelt by His Holy Spirit? Are you NOW fitting into His church as a fellow citizen and member of God's household? Are you NOW allowing God to demonstrate His manifold wisdom through you unto the principalities and powers in heavenly places? Are you NOW accepting His power and glory to work in you? Are you NOW walking worthy of the vocation to which you are called? Are you NOW following God by walking in the kind of love that Jesus demonstrated?

As you say yes to these questions you will grow into maturity (Ephesians 4:13-16), unto the stature of the fullness of Christ.

> "Till we all come to the unity of the faith and of the knowledge of the Son of God, to a perfect man, to the measure of the stature of the fullness of Christ; that we should no longer be children, tossed to and fro and carried about with every wind of doctrine, by the trickery of men, in the cunning craftiness of deceitful plotting, But, speaking the truth in love, may grow up in all things into Him who is the head—Christ— from whom the whole body, joined and knit together by what every joint supplies, according to the effective working by which every part does its share, causes growth of the body for the edifying of itself in love.

YOU WILL THEN LOOK LIKE JESUS!

I am told at times that my children look like me. They walk like me. They talk like me. They act like me. And at times they even think like me. Just as this is true on a human level, it can be true on a supernatural level. Through God's exceeding great and precious promises we are made to be partakers of His divine nature (2 Peter 1:4). According to John 15:1-8 and Matthew 7:16-20, Christ's life will produce fruit in us and identify us as His disciples.

> "I am the true vine, and My Father is the vinedresser. Every branch in Me that does not bear fruit He takes away; and every *branch* that bears fruit He prunes, that it may bear more fruit. You are already clean because of the word which I have spoken to you. Abide in Me, and I in you. As the branch cannot bear fruit of itself, unless it abides in the vine, neither can you, unless you abide in Me. I am the vine, you *are* the branches. He who abides in Me, and I in him, bears much fruit; for without Me you can do nothing. If anyone does not abide in Me, he is cast out as a branch and is withered; and they gather them and throw *them* into the fire, and they are burned. If you abide in Me, and My words abide in you, you will ask what you desire, and it shall be done for you. By this My Father is glorified, that you

bear much fruit; so you will be My disciples." John 15:1-8

"You will know them by their fruits. Do men gather grapes from thorn bushes or figs from thistles? Even so, every good tree bears good fruit, but a bad tree bears bad fruit. A good tree cannot bear bad fruit, nor *can* a bad tree bear good fruit. Every tree that does not bear good fruit is cut down and thrown into the fire. Therefore by their fruits you will know them." Matthew 7:16-20

Ephesians declares that we should not look like the devil as in our former life (2:2-3). We should not look like other gentiles who walk in the vanity of their mind (4:17-22). We should not look defiled by sinful practice (5:3-5). But rather, we should look like a new man (4:23-24). We should look like Christ (5:1-2). We should look like wise men (5:15). We should look like sober men (5:18). We should look like the family of God (6:1-5). As Christians we should look like Jesus because we also are sons of God. As Christians we should look like Jesus because we are His brothers. As Christians we should look like other Christians because we are members of the family of God.

Paul's previous use of the word "now" is accented by several other appeals, first and again to our time, then to the quality of its use.

"Redeeming the time, because the days are evil. Therefore do not be unwise, but understand what the will of the Lord *is*. And do not be drunk with wine, in which is dissipation; but be filled with the Spirit, speaking to one another in psalms and hymns and spiritual songs, singing and making melody in your heart to the Lord, giving thanks always for all things to God the Father in the name of our Lord Jesus Christ." Ephesians 5:16-20

As we know, time is fleeting. Though the word time has a number of Greek counterparts, here the word "kairos" can be particularly contrasted to "chronos", time here referring to a fixed or even special season as opposed to an uncertain or general period. It seems that the time allotted to each of us is as unique as we are. There are certain purposes designed for the slot that we fill. Perhaps this gives rise to sayings such as, "this is your time". Even though we are called generally to the same purposes and goals, we definitely have unique individual and corporate opportunities. The church in this last day's age of Pentecost is specially equipped to accomplish what others could not. Your individual role in the same has a similar accent. Though I stated at the onset that another should have written this book, I am compelled by this reasoning to put pen to paper as I am doing. This thought echoes Mordecai's appeal to Esther, "…who knows whether you have come to the kingdom for *such* a time as this?" Esther 4:14

Concerning the quality of time's use, if the days are evil, we have great opportunity to proclaim the goodness of God and display the same by walking in the works He has prepared for us. We would do well also to continually ask God for wisdom (v. 17), James 1:5-8 particularly applying here.

> "If any of you lacks wisdom, let him ask of God, who gives to all liberally and without reproach, and it will be given to him. But let him ask in faith, with no doubting, for he who doubts is like a wave of the sea driven and tossed by the wind. For let not that man suppose that he will receive anything from the Lord; *he is* a double-minded man, unstable in all his ways."

One of the most common questions Christians ask is, "How can I know God's will for my life?" There is no substitute for asking in faith. Presenting yourself continually available to God (consecration) is another key.

> "I beseech you therefore, brethren, by the mercies of God, that you present your bodies a living sacrifice, holy, acceptable to God, *which is* your reasonable service. And do not be conformed to this world, but be transformed by the renewing of your mind, that you may

prove what *is* that good and acceptable and perfect will of God." Romans 12:1-2

Ephesians 5:18 is cast in such a way as to suggest that we are to be excessively filled with the Spirit. This can only be another allusion to the Baptism in the Holy Spirit. God desires to overflow our lives into that of others. Hearts that are filled with worship, melody, joy, and thanksgiving round out the life of one who looks like Christ. No wonder Jesus drew the multitudes to Himself! Children likewise were blessed in His presence. This will be true of any who display His character.

Another aspect of Christ's relationship to the church now comes into play. It is a mystery. And it is illustrated by marriage.

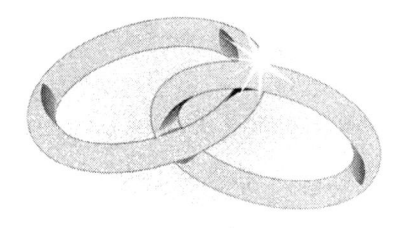

Chapter 14

"Heavenly Places and Beyond" Marriage Is Where It's At
Ephesians 5:21-6:9

When God created Adam He said, "...*It is* not good that man should be alone; I will make him a helper comparable to him" Genesis 2:18. The institution of marriage was born. A relationship was created through which God intended to illustrate His ultimate love for the church. What went wrong and what have been the effects? We need to more closely look at the fall of man and the resulting detour that marriage has taken to this present day.

In God's plan to prepare a people of His own, marriage was His first demonstration of purpose. It is related to us in Genesis.

"Then God said, "Let Us make man in Our image, according to Our likeness; let them have dominion over the fish of the sea, over the birds of the air, and over the cattle, over all the earth and over every creeping thing that creeps on the earth." So God created man in His *own* image; in the image of God He created him; male and female He created them. Then God blessed them, and God said to them, "Be fruitful and multiply; fill the earth and subdue it; have dominion over the fish of the sea, over the birds of the air, and over every living thing that moves on the earth." Genesis 1:26-28

"And the LORD God said, "*It is* not good that man should be alone; I will make him a helper comparable to him. And the LORD God caused a deep sleep to fall on Adam, and he slept; and He took one of his ribs, and closed up the flesh in its place. Then the rib which the LORD God had taken from man He made into a woman, and He brought her to the man. And Adam said: 'This *is* now bone of my bones And flesh of my flesh;She shall be called Woman, because she was taken out of Man.' Therefore a man shall leave his father and mother and be joined to his wife, and they shall become one flesh." Genesis 2:18, 21-24

When Jesus was questioned about the dissolution of marriage, he quoted and reinforced God's prescription for marriage.

"And He answered and said to them, 'Have you not read that He who made them at the beginning 'made them male and female,' and said, 'For this reason a man shall leave his father and mother and be joined to his wife, and the two shall become one flesh'? So then, they are no longer two but one flesh. Therefore what God has joined together, let not man separate." Matthew 19:4-6

But as with all other elements of the building process, man here too has a tremendous capacity to build apart from God. Simultaneous with man's alienation from God in Eden, man was alienated from his wife. Initially, their innocence was described as follows. "And they were both naked, the man and his wife, and were not ashamed." Genesis 2:25. Later, having become aware of himself, Adam stated. "...I heard Your voice in the garden, and I was afraid because I was naked; and I hid myself" Genesis 3:10. Adam and Eve were both ashamed. They hid themselves from God. They avoided responsibility for their sin by using blame. Adam blamed Eve. Eve in turn blamed the devil. Rationalization numbed the guilt of sin. Humanistic reasoning began a process that built something which resembled God's plan, but proved to be moving in a drastically different direction. A process unfolded which continues to this day, man trying to build families, civilizations, and ultimately the church with an alternate plan...a plan without the absolute foundation of marriage. A casual survey of biblical, secular and church history will establish a perspective.

Seven generations from Adam, Lamech abandoned God's plan of lifelong monogamy, "Then Lamech took for himself two wives..." Genesis 4:19. The history of Lamech is chronicled as short and corrupt. Around that time Adam begot another son, Seth, through whose descent the promised seed would come (Compare Genesis 3:15 and 4:25). Ultimately Methuselah was born of Seth's descendents and he begot another Lamech who in turn begot Noah, ten generations from Adam. By this time, man's condition had degenerated to a deplorable state and God was constrained to destroy all but Noah and his family (Genesis 6:5-8). God's intent was to produce a godly seed and marriage was the means of conveyance.

After the flood, the command was again to "Be fruitful and multiply, and fill the earth" (Genesis 9:1). At that time God made a covenant with Noah and his seed after him (Genesis 9:6-9).

"Whoever sheds man's blood, By man his blood shall be shed; For in the image of God He made man. And as for you, be fruitful and multiply; Bring forth abundantly in the earth and multiply in it." Then God spoke to Noah and to his sons with him, saying: "And as for Me, behold, I establish My covenant with you and with your descendants after you."

Interestingly, without mention of polygamy, Shem, Ham, and Japheth were the progenitors of the nations of the world. Subsequently, Abraham was born of the descendents of Shem. This further isolated the promised seed up to the time of Jacob. Though polygamy again appears in the life of Abraham and Jacob, God's grace remembers the promise to Abraham, and through Jacob's son Judah came David, and ultimately Christ.

Time does not permit us to at this time thoroughly trace the vast heartache and tragedy that the generations between Abraham and Christ experienced by deviating from God's absolute foundation of marriage. But certain notable events cannot be overlooked in the context of this discussion.

Not only did Jacob's polygamy complicate his circumstances and the subsequent history of Israel, but the effect of Esau's polygamy is pressing upon the Jews and Gentiles of the world up to this day. Secular and church history further reveals the devastating path of this pursuit. Nations have deteriorated and fallen as this and subsequent abhorrences such as adultery, incest and sodomy have developed. Where are the Egyptian, Babylonian, Greek, or Roman cultures today as compared to their former places in world influence? Comparable collapse can be traced among historical European monarchies. Although Eastern cultures are not illustrated in this discussion, modern civilizations are currently experiencing the effects of experimenting with God's plan for marriage, with AIDS being the most horrid example. Church history is also replete with the destructive consequences caused by the deterioration of marital absolutes.

Polygamy and its related mutations are not man's only deviation from God's plan of life long monogamy. Intermarriage contrary to God's design for the chosen seed has intermittently plagued God's purposes among men as well. Of note are Abraham and Hagar (an Egyptian), Ishamel as a progenitor of the Arabs, and Esau and his wives of Canaan. In the wilderness the Jews neared destruction as Balaam's doctrine caused the children of Israel to intermarry with the women of Moab (Numbers 25 and Revelation 2:14). Had it not been for the zeal of Phinehas (who stayed the plague by executing a Jewish man and Midianitish woman in the very act), the greater part of Israel may have been destroyed. As it was, twenty-four thousand died in the plague. Eventually, Israel was thrust out of the Promised Land and carried into captivity largely as a result of intermarriage and related idolatry with the Canaanites and surrounding nations.

Let it be observed at this point that God's grace was also woven into this tapestry of tragedy. His mercy was revealed in the blessings issued to Jacob's sons though born via polygamy. Ruth and Esther demonstrate how God's sovereignty works itself out in the darkest scenarios. Even David's moral failure did not preclude God's purpose to bring Christ to earth. But do not let God's grace and blessing cloud His desired will for us.

Entering the New Testament economy of things on this subject does not change the dismal state of affairs. The church, carrying the gospel of grace, finds that the sin twisted condition of man continues with a broken foundation of marriage. The Jews (who ought to have known better), the Samaritans, the aforementioned Greeks and Romans, and every modern nation suffer from the plague caused by foundations missing in marriage. And now the same has overtaken the church itself. Statistics of divorce and remarriage are quickly becoming comparable to those among the non-churched. And who will reverse the momentum? If the church does not, no one will. And how can the church do it? Only the establishment or relaying of new foundations will accomplish such a thing.

And yet, as could be predicted, the church is flooded today with a myriad of books, tapes, etc., rationalizing the continued need for divorce, remarriage and alternate lifestyles to satisfy/accommodate man's need. The fact is, it is getting worse. The church is already reeling from a misdirected generation of children who, being raised in the church, are victims of these philosophies.

Prayer must be made for God to raise up foundational ministries who will stay the plague as Phinehas once did. But prayer is not enough. Drastic...and I am sure even controversial action must be taken. Even since this writing commenced, we have witnessed the Institute in Basic Youth Conflicts, Focus On The Family, and others who have provided a measure of change. But there are also voices within the church that are avoiding hard solutions by proclaiming that God's mercy and love are sufficient for the need. A sense of resolve has been replaced by helplessness. "Our culture has gone too far". "You can't reverse marital and corresponding family breakdowns". "Fairness Theology" excuses the conditions of many broken marriages, divorces, and remarriages. The church has adjusted to our fallen culture instead of proving to be the ark that alone can save it. Through all the arguments and discussions of exception clauses, unchangeable circumstances after conversion, and complexities of modern civilizations, Jesus' words still ring true, "what, therefore, God has joined together, let not man put asunder" Matthew 19:6.

Paul, illustrating one's death to sin and union with Christ states,

> "For the woman who has a husband is bound by the law to *her* husband as long as he lives. But if the husband dies, she is released from the law of *her* husband. So then if, while *her* husband lives, she marries another man, she will be called an adulteress; but if her husband dies, she is free from that law, so that she is no adulteress, though she has married another man." Romans 7:2-3

Also, he ends his discussion on the regulations of marriage in 1 Corinthians 7 by declaring,

> "A wife is bound by law as long as her husband lives; but if her husband dies, she is at liberty to be married to whom she wishes, only in the Lord." 1 Corinthians 7:29

Again, voices today label this as legalism, or at least outdated and impractical. Arguments are also presented that insist that Paul had other situations in mind as he spoke, or that God's mercy and grace spoken of in other contexts must apply here because God forgives all sin and gives second chances. There are even those who go as far as saying that marriages "not made in heaven" are exempt from these principles and can be dissolved.

Scripture responds in Hebrews 13:4 by stating that "Marriage *is* honorable among all, and the bed undefiled; but fornicators and adulterers God will judge".

This generation has experienced the result of children being given sex education in the public schools accompanied by a permissive attitude. The result has been an increase in disease and illegitimate pregnancy that has touched most of our families. Is the church so blind to not see that interfering with foundations of absolutes in marriage is resulting in even greater confusion and sickness?

Now that we have viewed man's departure from God's plan and the effect upon the church, let us work back toward an understanding of God's solution that is set forth in Ephesians.

Considering again the original failure of Adam and Eve, things could have been different. Eve could have gone to Adam, or directly to God for that matter, and informed either of the serpent's proposition. Even after she had eaten the fruit she could have gone to Adam or God and found redemption.

God intended Adam to be a saving influence to Eve as much as He intended Eve to be an help for Adam. It was God's desire for them to walk in obedience and to grow in wisdom. It was not God's will for them to partake of the tree of the knowledge of good and evil. He wanted them to grow unto the measure of the stature of the fullness of Christ (Ephesians 4:13) by practicing two virtues that can best be applied in the marriage relationship. These are submission and love. We are again introduced to them in Ephesians 5:21-33. I have come to call them the impossible twins because apart from Divine enablement they are impossible to live out.

But the crucible of marriage provides us the opportunity to peer into the love relationship of Christ and His church. How great is His love for us. It is such that He desires to become one with us. Verses 31 and 32 of this passage indicate that the union first formed in Genesis was the initial revelation of the mystery that would ultimately come to be known as "...Christ in you, the hope of glory"

(Colossians 1:27). This mystery of the church potentially comes to light through the demonstration of love and submission in marriage.

First there is mutual submission, "Submitting to one another in the fear of God" (Ephesians 5:21). Yes, submitting to God makes sense in light of His position compared to ours. But Christ submitting to us appears implausible if not impossible, again, because of His position compared to ours! Yet the mystery begins to unfold with the Incarnation, Christ becoming man. By putting off His robes of glory, taking on the form of man, and becoming sin for us on the cross, Jesus portrayed ultimate submission to God (He chose the Father's will over His own) and man (by becoming the Servant of all). Jesus did this by Divine unction as a man.

How easy this should then be for us, except for the blemish of sin. Adam and Eve lived in harmony with one another and God. Sin changed all of that. Relationship with God was broken. Death entered. Adam and Eve were separated by shame and mistrust. Though plagued by pain of childbirth, Eve would yet desire her husband. But he would rule over her. And that tension of being unable to submit one to another because of sin plagues the institutions of marriage and the church to this day. And yet the mystery continues to unfold, Christ initiating...we responding. Though Paul first instructs the wife to submit to her husband (impossible!), a key is given, "...as unto the Lord" v.22. "We love him, because he first loved us" 1 John 4:19. Sin prevents a wife from submitting to her husband. Sin prevents the church from submitting to Jesus.

But Divine love changes all that. "But God demonstrates His own love toward us, in that while we were still sinners, Christ died for us" Romans 5:8. Submission means yielding. Yielding means trusting. Trusting means faith, which is resting on the ability of another to do what I am unable to do.

While I was in India, road traffic was impossible. The roads were unreasonably narrow in many places. Vehicles would be speeding toward one another on a road that would allow only one to continue. Something had to give. Someone had to yield. He who submitted was really submitting to a higher authority or principle, knowing that upon yielding he too would be able to pass. By yielding he saved himself from destruction and protected the other driver from the same.

Thus submission brings order, order to a marriage, and order to the church. When a wife submits to her husband "as unto the Lord" she is displaying trust in Christ, that He will make a way for her. Her submission allows her husband to proceed. When the church submits to Christ we are displaying trust in Christ, that He will make a way for us. Our submission allows Him to work out His perfect will for us. The impossible becomes possible because the curse of sin is broken.

> "I beseech you therefore, brethren, by the mercies of God, that you present your bodies a living sacrifice, holy, acceptable to God, *which is* your reasonable service. And do not be conformed to this world, but be transformed by the renewing of your mind, that you may prove what *is* that good and acceptable and perfect will of God" (Romans 12:1-2).

Yet underlying this work of submission, resulting in trust and grace, is the initiating work of love. Though Paul commands the husband to love his wife (impossible!), another key is given, "...just as Christ also loved the church and gave Himself for her". Human love is plagued by sin, resulting in self-service and an unending path of destruction. Sin prevents a man from loving beyond a human level. Sin prevents a man from loving his wife. Sin prevents a man from loving God. Adam said, "...I was afraid because I was naked; and I hid myself " Genesis 3:10.

But Divine love again changes that.

> "And we have known and believed the love that God has for us. God is love, and he who abides in love abides in God, and God in him. Love has been perfected among us in this: that we may have boldness in the day of judgment; because as He is, so are we in this world. There is no fear in love; but perfect love casts out fear, because fear involves torment. But he who fears has not been made perfect in love. We love Him because He first loved us." (1 John 4:16-19.

The mystery then unfolds, that is concerning Christ and the church. Christ loves us. We submit to Christ. The two shall be one flesh. Because of our union with Christ John is able to say, "...because as He is, so are we in this world". Or as Paul says in Colossians 1:27

> "To them God willed to make known what are the riches of the glory of this

mystery among the Gentiles: which is Christ in you, the hope of glory."

The original premise and title of this book *"You Are The Temple"* reaches a high water mark with the revelation of this mystery. We can speak about God's love all that we want. But until we know how to apply it in the most basic human relationships (marriage and family) we indeed reflect what Paul wrote in 1 Corinthians 13:1.

"Though I speak with the tongues of men and of angels, but have not love, I have become sounding brass or a clanging cymbal."

Several challenges emerge from these considerations. First, will the church once again accept marriage as God's foundational institution for the human race? Next, will the church accept the responsibility for modeling Christ-centered marriage to a lost and dying world? Both of these depend on this last challenge. Will present members of the church return to a sacred/biblical model of marriage and forsake the humanistic models that are vying for predominance?

These challenges can be answered when ministers of the gospel will once again proclaim God's plan of life-long monogamy. Many ministers feel trapped here because of the preponderance of divorced people in our society. Our culture and laws, which only "include" ministers among a list of marrying agents, complicates this. Options are limited to civil or religious ceremonies. No fault divorce laws have replaced the biblical model previously discussed. Adultery is no longer enforced as a criminal offence in our civil system. Hence, though the stigma of divorce continues to plague remarriage and family structure, the church (and ministers as marrying agents) is pressured to go with the flow.

But church members at large have an opportunity to respond to these challenges by choosing to lay down their lives and self interest for the sake of future generations. This will involve once again viewing marriage as a sacred institution, ordained by God. Seeing marriage as a God-ordained covenant rather than as an option in a pluralistic culture will restore accountability to the institution of marriage. Then there is the choice of remarriage while a former spouse is living. If one generation within the church would choose to forsake this practice, the scriptural plan of life-long monogamy could be restored to the church. In turn, we could then offer our children and a broken world an example of what God intends for all. The beauty of God- sanctioned marriage will not only provide greater opportunities for the church to grow into Christ's image, but will also by its very nature proclaim the gospel to a lost and dying world.

Paul's final words to the Ephesians then extend the principles of submission and love into family and social arenas, children obeying and honoring parents, fathers bringing up children in the nurture and admonition of the Lord, even slaves and their owners (what we have come to see, and rightly so, as an unacceptable human relationship) living in harmony under God. This is possible in a fallen world when the Kingdom of God is ruling in the hearts of men. But it also reminds us that we are not complete yet.

Perhaps the greatest challenge facing the generation of the church that embraces Christ's return is to rediscover God's plan for marriage and family. The influence of humanism throughout the world continues trying to restrict a godly seed through its false precepts of over-population, homosexuality, abortion, adultery, fornication, rationalized divorce and remarriage, infanticide, euthanasia, and even suicide. Rather, God desires mankind to **"Be fruitful and** multiply, and fill the earth" through the institution of life-long monogamy Genesis 9:1. This command has never been rescinded. God also desires the church to multiply and represent His Kingdom during this age and the ages to come. Marriage is His chosen institution which provides a living picture of Christ and the church. It in turn gives birth to families/households that when redeemed, result in a microcosm of the church during this age. God is, and always has been, rooting for a redeemed mankind. This is our created purpose.

> "For the earnest expectation of the creation eagerly waits for the revealing of the sons of God" Romans 8:19.
> "And now, little children, abide in Him, that when He appears, we may have confidence and not be ashamed before Him at His coming. If you know that He is righteous, you know that everyone who practices righteousness is born of Him. Behold what manner of love the Father has bestowed on us, that we should be called children of God! Therefore the world does not know us, because it did not know Him. Beloved, now we are children of God; and it has not yet been revealed what we shall be, but we know that when He is revealed, we shall be

like Him, for we shall see Him as He is" 1 John 2:28-3:2.

Until then we are engaged in a cosmic battle, one that Ephesians earlier depicted as occurring in heavenly places, that now requires us to don supernatural armaments and tactics.

Chapter 15

"Heavenly Places and Beyond" We are In a War
Ephesians 6:10-24

Ephesians begins by registering the church in heavenly places (1:3). The church can then live out its potential through on-going enlightenment (1:18) as a result of prayer. The choice is ours. It could be argued that no generation of the church has experienced that potential since the book of Acts was recorded. However, those of us privileged to live during the modern Pentecostal out-pouring could be on the threshold of the greatest and last Holy Spirit deluge. Scripture points to such a climax.

"'And it shall come to pass in the last days, says God, That I will pour out of My Spirit on all flesh; Your sons and your daughters shall prophesy, Your young men shall see visions, Your old men shall dream dreams. And on My menservants and on My maidservantsI will pour out My Spirit in those days; And they shall prophesy.
I will show wonders in heaven above
And signs in the earth beneath:
Blood and fire and vapor of smoke.
The sun shall be turned into darkness, And the moon into blood, Before the coming of the great and awesome day of the LORD. And it shall come to pass That whoever calls on the name of the LORD Shall be saved.'"

When Peter quoted Joel's prophecy on the day of Pentecost, two aspects of it were not fully realized. The "last days" will ultimately and obviously be fulfilled by the generation that is present at the return of Jesus. Likewise, the "all flesh" portion of that prophecy is nearer then ever before with this gospel being preached virtually in all nations.

There are also several obscure references woven in the midst of Habakkuk's prophecy which point to a great last days out-pouring. First is the reference to an appointed vision at the end (2:2-3).

"Then the LORD answered me and said:
'Write the vision And make *it* plain on tablets, That he may run who reads it. For the vision *is* yet for an appointed time; But at the end it will speak, and it will not lie. Though it tarries, wait for it; Because It will surely come, It will not tarry.'"

Second is that bedrock of Paul's theology that was restored to the church via the Reformation, "…but the just shall live by his faith. " (2:4). And third is the reference that applies here, "For the earth shall be filled with the knowledge of the glory of the Lord, as the waters cover the sea" (2:14).

How shall this be accomplished? It unfolds when Paul's final instructions to the Ephesians are effectively realized by the church. "Finally, my brethren, be strong in the Lord, and in the power of his might" Ephesians 6:10. The first admonition of Jesus to the seven Asian churches in Revelation is pointed to Ephesus's loss of its first love. The church that received the highest written revelation of Christ's presence, power, and work was the first to be corrected. Walking in the midst of the candlesticks, Jesus threatened the removal of His presence if they did not repent. The metaphor of the candlesticks as the churches clearly is a reference to the presence of the Holy Spirit in the churches. Old Testament typology refers to this as well, culminating with Zechariah's connection of the seven lamps and the Holy Spirit (Zechariah 4:1-6).

Now the angel who talked with me came back and wakened me, as a man who is wakened out of his sleep. And he said to me, "What do you see?" So I said, "I am looking, and there *is* a lampstand of solid gold with a bowl on top of it, and on the *stand* seven lamps with seven pipes to the seven lamps. Two olive trees *are* by it, one at the right of the bowl and the other at its left." So I answered and spoke to the angel who talked with me, saying, "What *are* these, my lord?" Then the angel who talked with me answered and said to me, "Do you not know what these are?" And I said, "No, my lord." So he answered and said to me: " This *is* the word of the LORD to Zerubbabel: 'Not by might nor by power, but by My Spirit,' Says the LORD of hosts.

Christ's gospel teaching about the wise virgins who kept a supply of oil at hand until the bridegroom's appearance also substantiates this concept.

"Then the kingdom of heaven shall be likened to ten virgins who took their lamps and went out to meet the bridegroom. Now five of them were wise, and five *were* foolish. Those who *were* foolish took their lamps and took no oil with them, but the wise took oil in their vessels with their lamps. But while the bridegroom was delayed, they all slumbered and slept.

"And at midnight a cry was *heard:*'Behold, the bridegroom is coming; go out to meet him!' Then all those virgins arose and trimmed their lamps. And the foolish said to the wise, 'Give us *some* of your oil, for our lamps are going out.' But the wise answered, saying, '*No,* lest there should not be enough for us and you; but go rather to those who sell, and buy for yourselves.' And while they went to buy, the bridegroom came, and those who were ready went in with him to the wedding; and the door was shut. "Afterward the other virgins came also, saying, 'Lord, Lord, open to us!' But he answered and said, 'Assuredly, I say to you, I do not know you.' "Watch therefore, for you know neither the day nor the hour in which the Son of Man is coming."

And so, we must know what it means to "...strong in the Lord, and in the power of his might". It can mean nothing less than walking in that same anointing that Jesus walked in, living out the "greater works" that Jesus said would be done because He goes to the Father.

> Nevertheless I tell you the truth. It is to your advantage that I go away; for if I do not go away, the Helper will not come to you; but if I depart, I will send Him to you." John 16:7.

The "Promised One" is referenced in different contexts but is always speaking of the Holy Spirit.

> "Behold, I send the Promise of My Father upon you; but tarry in the city of Jerusalem until you are endued with power from on high." Luke 24:49.

> "But you shall receive power when the Holy Spirit has come upon you; and you shall be witnesses to Me in Jerusalem, and in all Judea and Samaria, and to the end of the earth." Acts 1:8.

> "Therefore being exalted to the right hand of God, and having received from the Father the promise of the Holy

Spirit, He poured out this which you now see and hear." Acts 2:33

"Then Peter said to them, 'Repent, and let every one of you be baptized in the name of Jesus Christ for the remission of sins; and you shall receive the gift of the Holy Spirit. For the promise is to you and to your children, and to all who are afar off, as many as the Lord our God will call.'" Acts 2:38-39

Though the words "might" and "power" in Ephesians 6:10 are not the dunamis of Luke 24 and Acts 1, the exhortation to "be strong" is derived from dunamis. Strong's Concordance indicates that the preposition "en" connected with "dunamoo" denotes a fixed position and instrumentality. [vii] In other words we are to remain or abide in that position of the Lord's explosive power, might, and dominion. Earlier references to "dunamis" in Ephesians provide immediate and greater context, thus concluding that Paul is making direct reference to the power emanating from the baptism of the Holy Spirit.

"And what *is* the exceeding greatness of His power toward us who believe, according to the working of His mighty power which He worked in Christ when He raised Him from the dead and seated *Him* at His right hand in the heavenly *places,* far above all principality and power and might and dominion, and every name that is named, not only in this age but also in that which is to come." Ephesians 1:19-21

"Of which I became a minister according to the gift of the grace of God given to me by the effective working of His power." Ephesians 3:7
"Now to Him who is able to do exceedingly abundantly above all that we ask or think, according to the power that works in us, to Him *be* glory in the church by Christ Jesus to all generations, forever and ever. Amen." Ephesians 3:20-21

It is only this miraculous power (dunamis), associated with Holy Spirit baptism, that will bring glory in the church by Christ Jesus to all generations. Though the baptism of the Holy Spirit was addressed earlier under "Your Position In Christ", further discussion is necessary before this presentation can conclude. Sadly, our Pentecostal churches (at least in the West) are filled with people who have not yet experienced the baptism of the Holy Spirit or who have long since ceased to walk in His fullness.

Jesus commanded the apostles to wait for His promise.

"And being assembled together with *them,* He commanded them not to depart from Jerusalem, but to wait for the Promise of the Father, "which," *He said,* "you have heard from Me; for John truly baptized with water, but you shall be baptized with the Holy Spirit not many days from now." (Acts 1:4-5),

Paul's conclusion is that we must live in the Lord's mighty power. It stands on the premise that Jesus has won the war. It is our privilege and responsibility to appropriate what He has accomplished. Four admonitions emerge from this knowledge.

First, we must define our battlefield. Who has the higher ground? Without a doubt, we do! However, much of our struggle is keeping this in focus. Satan would like us to believe that he owns the earth, that he controls the heavenly sphere, that we are the intruders of his realm. Nothing could be further from the truth. Jesus created and owns everything. He is Lord over all.

"He has put all *things* under His feet, and gave Him *to be* head over all *things* to the church, which is His body, the fullness of Him who fills all in all. Ephesians 1:22-23.

He brings His Kingdom rule wherever His servants will declare it. "The time is fulfilled, and the kingdom of God is at hand. Repent, and believe in the gospel." Mark 1:15 This should be the battle cry of all who have put on Christ. All who are indwelt by the Holy Spirit, possessing the same anointing of Christ, should proclaim in his stead,

"...I will build My church, and the gates of Hades shall not prevail against it" Matthew 16:18.

"And to make all see what *is* the fellowship of the mystery, which from the beginning of the ages has been hidden in God who created all things through Jesus Christ; to the intent that now the manifold wisdom of God might be made known by the church to the principalities and powers in the heavenly *places,* according to the eternal purpose which He accomplished in Christ Jesus our Lord, in whom we have boldness and access with confidence through faith in Him." Ephesians 3:9-12).

Truly, the best defense emerges through the best offence. Because we have the upper ground we must unrelentingly attack the enemy, destroying his works both within and without and on every hand!

Secondly, we must know our resources. We've already established that they are found in the Lord's strength and the power of His might. But let's go further, again referring to Mark's account.

"It came to pass in those days *that* Jesus came from Nazareth of Galilee, and was baptized by John in the Jordan.

And immediately, coming up from the water, He saw the heavens parting and the Spirit descending upon Him like a dove. Then a voice came from heaven, 'You are My beloved Son, in whom I am well pleased.'... Then they were all amazed, so that they questioned among themselves, saying, 'What is this? What new doctrine *is* this? For with authority He commands even the unclean spirits, and they obey Him'....But that you may know that the Son of Man has power on earth to forgive sins—He said to the paralytic, 'I say to you, arise, take up your bed, and go to your house.'" Mark 1:9-11,27; 2:10

Christ's authority is vested in us as His ambassadors.

This applies to our mission and to our power. And then it extends to our armament. The whole armor of God is ours! Like David, we do not have to trust in the arm of flesh or another man's armor. Again, like David to Goliath, we come not with a sword, spear, and a shield but "...in the name of the Lord of hosts, the God of the armies of Israel..." 1 Samuel 17:45.

What is the armament of God? It goes beyond the list of Ephesians 6:11-ff. It is indeed the whole armor. All the resources of heaven are at our disposal. Truly,

> "...the weapons of our warfare *are* not carnal but mighty in God for pulling down strongholds, casting down arguments and every high thing that exalts itself against the knowledge of God, bringing every thought into captivity to the obedience of Christ" 2 Corinthians 10:4-5.

Honestly, I don't believe the church has yet experienced the fullness of what this all means. I know that I have not. That is why the effort continues to deserve our attention.

> "Now unto him that is able to do exceeding abundantly above all that we ask our think, according to the power that works in us, unto him be glory in the church by Christ Jesus throughout all ages, world without end. Amen" Ephesians 3:20-21.

Thirdly, we must identify the enemy. Mark 3:23-27 sees Jesus shift the accusation that He derived His power from the devil to a discussion of a kingdom divided against itself.

> "So He called them to *Himself* and said to them in parables: "How can Satan cast out Satan? If a kingdom is divided against itself, that kingdom cannot

stand. And if a house is divided against itself, that house cannot stand. And if Satan has risen up against himself, and is divided, he cannot stand, but has an end. No one can enter a strong man's house and plunder his goods, unless he first binds the strong man. And then he will plunder his house."

Two thoughts emerge from this process. Satan and his forces, not flesh and blood, are our primary foe (Ephesians 6:12).

"For we do not wrestle against flesh and blood, but against principalities, against powers, against the rulers of the darkness of this age, against spiritual *hosts* of wickedness in the heavenly *place.*"

Also, Kingdom power is issued through Kingdom unity, which requires on-going discernment and introspection on our part. Mark 8:31-38 illustrates that through Peter's susceptibility to Satan's wiles, our flesh must daily be put to death.

"And He began to teach them that the Son of Man must suffer many things, and be rejected by the elders and chief priests and scribes, and be killed, and after three days rise again. He spoke this word openly. Then Peter took Him aside and began to rebuke Him. But when He had turned around and looked at His disciples, He rebuked Peter, saying, 'Get behind Me, Satan! For you are not mindful of the things of God, but the things of men.' When He had called the people to *Himself,* with His disciples also, He said to them, 'Whoever desires to come after Me, let him deny himself, and take up his cross, and follow Me. For whoever desires to save his life will lose it, but whoever loses his life for My sake and the gospel's will save it. For what will it profit a man if he gains the whole world, and loses his own soul? Or what will a man give in exchange for his soul? For whoever is ashamed of Me and My words in this adulterous and sinful generation, of him the Son of Man also will be ashamed when He comes in the glory of His Father with the holy angels.'"

Peter later admonishes us that steadfast vigilance and resistance to Satan's wiles is required among our brotherhood of saints, because the enemy's attacks are both universal and unrelenting (1 Peter 5:8-9).

"Be sober, be vigilant; because your adversary the devil walks about like a roaring lion, seeking whom he may devour. Resist him, steadfast in the faith, knowing that the same sufferings are experienced by your brotherhood in the world."

Some of our greatest setbacks continue to come from the sinful failures of saints. Nevertheless, we can and must stand, knowing that by faith we "…will be able to quench all the fiery darts of the wicked one." Ephesians 6:16, and that "…the God of all grace, who called us to His eternal glory by Christ Jesus, after you have suffered a while, perfect, establish, strengthen, and settle *you*" 1 Peter 5:10. Resisting the devil and repenting of all that the carnal mind presents will not only keep the enemy at bay, but continually enable us to advance the cause of the Kingdom.

Finally, we must take action. "Being strong, putting on, wrestling, taking, standing, praying" all refer to our constant activity. Because the battle is the Lord's, what might appear as inactivity is potentially our greatest course of action. Resting, obeying, patient waiting, listening, and the like, are all examples of activity that often result in mighty demonstrations of God's sovereign intervention. Taken together, John's record of Jesus example provides the key, "My Father has been working until now, and I have been working." (John 5:17).

Jesus' activity in Mark's gospel surely reveals how to take action. He was always inviting others to follow Him "Then Jesus said to them, "Follow Me, and I will make you become fishers of men." (1:17), directly speaking to the enemy "But Jesus rebuked him, saying, "Be quiet, and come out of him!" (1:25), proclaiming the promises of the Kingdom "When Jesus saw their faith, He said to the paralytic, 'Son, your sins are forgiven you.'" (2:5), taking the battle to the enemy "Then they came to the other side of the sea, to the country of the Gadarenes." (5:1), and being actively aware of God's power in His life "And Jesus, immediately knowing in Himself that power had gone out of Him, turned around in the crowd and said, 'Who touched My clothes?'" (5:30). Though "...we have been saved through faith... we are His workmanship, created in Christ Jesus for good works, which God prepared beforehand that we should walk in them." Ephesians 2:8, 10.

What is the greatest work of the church? An evangelist that I highly respect insists that winning the lost must always be first and foremost on our agenda. Of course we would expect that to be the battle cry of the evangelist. And who can argue that it must be a top priority. Loving God with all of our heart, soul, mind and strength, and loving your neighbor as yourself (Mark 12:30-31)...along with being conformed to the image of Jesus (Romans 8:29) are certainly high on that list as well. And prayer somehow must be found in the midst of all this activity. Yet Jesus said, "...This is the work of God, that you believe in Him whom He sent." John 6:29 Somewhere in Paul's appeal to "...be strong in the Lord and in the power of His might" there must be a shift from our ability to Christ's ability. It is predicated upon our willingness to forsake the flesh, as noble as it can appear, and to abide in the strength of Christ.

Paul's third (and last) prayer for the Ephesians (6:18-20) is actually an appeal to all of us to remember that this war will be won on our knees.

> "Praying always with all prayer and supplication in the Spirit, being watchful to this end with all perseverance and supplication for all the saints— and for me, that utterance may be given to me, that I may open my mouth boldly to make known the mystery of the gospel, for which I am an ambassador in chains; that in it I may speak boldly, as I ought to speak."

What are some of the things that should be central to our prayers? Consider the following.

We need to pray in the Spirit to ultimately bring about God's plan.

> "Likewise the Spirit also helps in our weaknesses. For we do not know what we should pray for as we ought, but the Spirit Himself makes intercession for us with groanings which cannot be uttered. Now He who searches the hearts knows what the mind of the Spirit *is*, because He makes intercession for the saints according to *the will of* God." Romans 8:26-27

"...nevertheless not My will, but Yours, be done" (Luke 22:42) was the ultimate example of our High Priest's instruction to His disciples, "...Your will be done On earth as *it is* in heaven" (Luke 11:2). It is surely related to Paul's first prayer for enlightenment (1:16-ff). As the church, we are fighting for the souls of men. Persevering prayer, supplication in the Spirit, and watching for all saints will ultimately unfold God's plan in our midst.

I will always be indebted to those who have modeled prayer in my life. One Sunday morning, during the busyness of bus ministry and preparation for Sunday School, I knocked on pastor Rowland Dean's office door. I'll never forget the literal glow on his face as he answered the door coming from his place of prayer. Another time, while accompanying pastor Wilbert Johnson on a hospital visit, I heard him unashamedly praying in tongues (as was his pattern) before he spoke healing in the name of Jesus. While serving an internship with pastor Chuck Skaggs, he invited me to daily spend the first hours of his schedule waiting on God in prayer. Spiritual warfare is best caught rather than taught. Modeling prayer is essential to the training and discipling process, and hence the work of the church. Jesus "...is also able to save to the uttermost those who come to God through Him, since He always lives to make intercession for them" Hebrews 7:25.

Though the Spirit severally distributes the gifts as He wills, the unction that comes from His presence and manifests as utterance and power is birthed and released via prayer.

> "Most assuredly, I say to you, he who believes in Me, the works that I do he will do also; and greater *works* than these he will do, because I go to My Father. And whatever you ask in My name, that I will do, that the Father may be glorified in the Son. If you ask

anything in My name, I will do *it*." John 14:12-14

"And whatever things you ask in prayer, believing, you will receive." Matthew 21:22

We have been asking Jesus to build His church in the community where we currently reside. In the 100 plus years of its existence, this community has never had a functioning, full gospel expression of the church. Much of our role has been to tear down strongholds through prayer and summon a spiritual awakening in the hearts of men. The fact is, in any community, foreign or abroad, someone must answer the call to stand in the gap before a harvest can come forth. Paul requested prayer for utterance and boldness (Ephesians 6:19).

"And for me, that utterance may be given to me, that I may open my mouth boldly to make known the mystery of the gospel."

Jesus told His disciples that they were reaping where others had labored (John 4:38).

"I sent you to reap that for which you have not labored; others have labored, and you have entered into their labors."

Certainly included was the labor of prayer. Prayer precedes evangelism and harvest. Discipleship raises up prayer warriors.

> "So then neither he who plants is anything, nor he who waters, but God who gives the increase. Now he who plants and he who waters are one, and each one will receive his own reward according to his own labor.
> For we are God's fellow workers; you are God's field, *you are* God's building."
> I Corinthians 3:7-9

Two more aspects of prayer will round out this discussion: ministering Christ's presence and faithful obedience. Paul here referred to himself as an ambassador in bonds (6:20). This brings to mind the fact that we too are Christ's ambassadors (2 Corinthians 5:20). "Now then, we are ambassadors for Christ, as though God were pleading through us: we implore *you* on Christ's behalf, be reconciled to God." But really, more is taking place than us representing Christ. His presence is actually with us and in us…if we will walk in that prayerful anointing. Though it was discussed earlier, Paul's testimony to the Corinthians was that he ministered "…not with persuasive words of human wisdom, but in demonstration of the Spirit and of power," (1 Corinthians 2:4). He told the Philippians that he desired to know Christ in the "…the power of His resurrection, and the fellowship of His sufferings, being conformed to His death" (Philippians 3:10). He knew that even though he was in bonds "…the word of

God is not chained" (2 Timothy 2:9). It was the church's prayers that brought angelic deliverance to Peter who was in jail (Acts 12). It is the prayers of the church that will bring the power of the gospel to break the bonds of sin and the chains of the devil that bind men's souls.

Chapter 16

PostScript
"Heavenly Places and Beyond"
A Final Review of the
Ephesian Church

The story line in Scripture is sometimes spotty at best. The history of the church at Ephesus is like that. From Acts 18:18-ff, its beginning and progression was quite eclectic. Arriving there with his companions Priscilla and Aquila, Paul appeared to just be passing through on his way back to Jerusalem for an upcoming feast. Little is said of his ministry there at that time, other than he entered into the synagogue...reasoned with the Jews...consented not to remain at their request because of his desire to get to Jerusalem by the feast time…promising, God willing, to return.

Apparently Priscilla and Aquila remained there and connected with Apollos when he later arrived. Interestingly, Apollos may not even have become a Christian yet. It was through Priscilla and Aquila that he advanced in his knowledge of the gospel and in turn began mightily preaching Jesus as the Christ. Later he was found in Achaia and then in Corinth where Paul had originally met Priscilla and Aquila. With Apollos in Corinth, Paul had now returned to Ephesus.

Let us pause to consider that there was an extensive amount of movement and interaction among the disciples who were instrumental in seeing the church born at Ephesus. In reality, it is very similar to what happens today. Jesus sovereignly is building His church through His servants in a manner that pleases Him. Seldom does one enter into an area where the ground has not been prepared or worked by another. Certainly God goes before by revealing Himself and drawing souls to Himself. We have opportunities to fulfill our roles.

> "For when one says, 'I am of Paul,' and another, 'I *am* of Apollos,' are you not carnal? Who then is Paul, and who *is* Apollos, but ministers through whom you believed, as the Lord gave to each one? I planted, Apollos watered, but God gave the increase. So then neither he who plants is anything, nor he who waters, but God who gives the increase. Now he who plants and he who waters

are one, and each one will receive his own reward according to his own labor. For we are God's fellow workers; you are God's field, you are God's building. According to the grace of God which was given to me, as a wise master builder I have laid the foundation, and another builds on it. But let each one take heed how he builds on it. For no other foundation can anyone lay than that which is laid, which is Jesus Christ." 1 Corinthians 3:4-11

This is mostly different from how the church views ministry today. Individuals are prone to get the credit and exalted above their brethren when harvest occurs, forgetting that "Unless the LORD builds the house, They labor in vain who build it" Psalm 127:1 (a).

Again considering Ephesus's history, Paul's return resulted in the disciples' water baptism in the name of the Lord...progressing from John's baptism to Christ's and ultimately to the baptism in the Holy Spirit. This all came about from the diverse ministry of Paul, Apollos, Priscilla and Aquila...five-fold ministers who demonstrated the headship of Jesus. But the story does not end there.

Discipleship continued for months in the face of strong opposition. Then two years passed with all of Asia hearing the gospel as a result of what was taking place in Ephesus. A riot culminated that period with Paul again traveling beyond Ephesus throughout Macedonia. But between the lines it is noted that a growing body of ministers was being raised up, among whom were Timothy, Erastus, Sopater, Aristarchus,

Secundus, Gaius, Tychicus, and Trophimus. Some were from Ephesus; some from scattered places throughout Macedonia. But interestingly, without fanfare or even details given, a body of elders also had come into existence in the church at Ephesus. While making what appeared to be his final journey through that region, Paul called for those elders to meet him in Miletus.

What happens next is vitally important to our understanding of this history, Paul's letter to the Ephesians, Jesus' message to that church in Revelation 2, and our mission for the 21st century and beyond. Will we embrace this and other New Testament examples of church life, or will we build as they did at Babel? Paul's final exhortation to the Ephesian elders (Acts 19:18-35) is truly an admonition to us as well.

> "And when they had come to him, he said to them: "You know, from the first day that I came to Asia, in what manner I always lived among you, serving the Lord with all humility, with many tears and trials which happened to me by the plotting of the Jews; how I kept back nothing that was helpful, but proclaimed it to you, and taught you publicly and from house to house, testifying to Jews, and also to Greeks, repentance toward God and faith toward our Lord Jesus Christ. And see, now I go bound in the spirit to Jerusalem, not knowing the things that will happen to me there,

except that the Holy Spirit testifies in every city, saying that chains and tribulations await me. But none of these things move me; nor do I count my life dear to myself, so that I may finish my race with joy, and the ministry which I received from the Lord Jesus, to testify to the gospel of the grace of God. "And indeed, now I know that you all, among whom I have gone preaching the kingdom of God, will see my face no more. Therefore I testify to you this day that I *am* innocent of the blood of all *men*. For I have not shunned to declare to you the whole counsel of God. Therefore take heed to yourselves and to all the flock, among which the Holy Spirit has made you overseers, to shepherd the church of God which He purchased with His own blood. For I know this, that after my departure savage wolves will come in among you, not sparing the flock. Also from among yourselves men will rise up, speaking perverse things, to draw away the disciples after themselves. Therefore watch, and remember that for three years I did not cease to warn everyone night and day with tears. "So now, brethren, I commend you to God and to the word of His grace, which is able to build you up and give you an inheritance among all those who are sanctified. I have coveted no one's silver or gold or apparel. Yes, you yourselves know that these hands have provided for my necessities, and for those who were with me. I have shown you in every way, by laboring like this, that you must support the weak. And remember the words of the Lord Jesus, that He said, 'It is more blessed to give than to receive.'"

Consider a few highlights of his message. Above all it was rooted in loving relationship, not programs, methods, or structure. It reflected about the time spent publicly and from house to house centered on repentance and faith toward the Lord Jesus Christ. It had little if anything to do with buildings and budgets, though they did not speak against them. Humility, tears, temptations and trials were remembered with great joy. Also called to remembrance was the necessity to declare all the counsel of God, attendance to personal spiritual welfare, oversight and feeding the church. This oversight was left in the hands of a group of men, not a single pastor. Reference was made that those from without (itinerate ministers?) as well as local disciples would give cause for constant vigilance. But clear confidence was also proclaimed in God's care and the word of his grace which was able to build them up and give them an inheritance among all that are sanctified. This was culminated by a quote from Jesus Himself, "It is more blessed to give that to receive".

The fact has been stated once and again, Jesus will build His church and the gates of hell will not prevail against it. He who addressed the Ephesian church in Revelation still walks in the midst of the candlesticks. He walks in our midst and His Spirit yet speaks to our direction and change. Will we respond accordingly?

I have not written this book because I have been successful. Ultimately only God will reveal that at His Judgment Seat. I have written it because God's word deserves on-going evaluation and application to our structure and methods. My prayer is that any influenced by this writing will likewise be motivated to contribute as they are graced by God.

"Till we all come in the unity of the faith, and of the knowledge of the Son of God, unto a perfect man, unto the measure of the stature of the fullness of Christ till we all come to the unity of the faith and of the knowledge of the Son of God, to a perfect man, to the measure of the stature of the fullness of Christ" Ephesians 4:13.

After all, *You Are The Temple.*

[i] Minutes of the 53rd Session of The General Council of the Assemblies of God, Convened in Orlando, Florida August 4-7, 2009, with Revised Constitution and Bylaws, p. 90

[ii] Minutes of the 53rd Session of The General Council of the Assemblies of God, Convened in Orlando, Florida August 4-7, 2009, with Revised Constitution and Bylaws, p. 100

[iii] Minutes of the 50th Session of The General Council of the Assemblies of God, Convened in Washington, D.C., July 31-August 3, 2003, with Revised Constitution and Bylaws

[iv] An Expository Dictionary of New Testament Words, W. E. Vine, M.A., Fleming H Revell Company, Old Tappan, New Jersey, 1966, Vol. II E-Li, p.209

[v] An Expository Dictionary of New Testament Words, W. E. Vine, M.A., Fleming H Revell Company, Old Tappan, New Jersey, 1966, Vol. II E-Li, p.259

[vi] An Expository Dictionary of New Testament Words, W. E. Vine, M.A., Fleming H Revell Company, Old Tappan, New Jersey, 1966, Vol. II E-Li, pp. 170-171

[vii] The New Strong's Exhaustive Concordance of the Bible, Thomas Nelson Publishers, 1990, A Concise Dictionary of the words in The Greek Testament, p. 28

CPSIA information can be obtained at www.ICGtesting.com
Printed in the USA
BVOW030123260413

319167BV00002B/4/P

9 781612 155005